The Old Farmer's Almanac
Book of Everyday Advice

THE OLD FARMER'S ALMANAC
Book of Everyday Advice

Judson D. Hale, Sr.

Editor

RANDOM HOUSE • NEW YORK

ISBN: 0-679-43673-1

To Sally
— *who has, thank goodness,*
never taken any of my advice seriously
since our marriage in 1958
and who has, in turn, invariably been
on target with hers.

Acknowledgments

THANKS FIRST AND FOREMOST must go to Sharon Smith, who took on my huge pile of folders, overflowing with a totally confusing assortment of papers and scribblings and, from that mess, produced this book. Also, thanks to David Rosenthal at Random House for his creative thoughts prior to my beginning this project — and for breakfast; to Jill Shaffer for all the design and art direction; to Sarah Hale for the art research; to Helen Marra, production manager at Random House; and to Almanac group publisher John Pierce and Almanac managing editor Susan Peery for invaluable advice and consultations from the beginning discussions to the final deadline.

I also would like to thank the following: Cathy Behrens for inputting the manuscript on disk; Ann Duffy for securing permissions; Barbara Jatkola for copyediting, fact checking, and proofreading; and Linda Ottavi for production assistance.

Finally, thanks to my golden retriever, Jeepers, who chewed up two chapters of material I'd spread out on the floor next to my desk one morning. Judging from her expression later, I'd have to say it wasn't particularly *good* advice anyway.

Contents

INTRODUCTION x

PART ONE: ADVICE FOR YOUR HOME 1

  1   In the Privacy of the Bedroom 2

  2   From Soup to the Kitchen Sink 32

  3   Around the Dining Room Table 54

  4   For the Room We Called the Parlor 72

  5   Out in the Garden 86

PART TWO: ADVICE FOR YOUR LIFE 105

  6   Those Carefree Childhood Years 106

  7   Facing Marriage, Family & Career 130

  8   Those Busy Middle Years 150

  9   Retirement & the Golden Times 174

 10   Old Age: Days of Wisdom & Reflection 192

Introduction

I'M PRETTY SURE THE BEST ADVICE I've ever received (so far) was from my uncle, the late Robb Sagendorph, the eleventh editor of *The Old Farmer's Almanac* and the man I succeeded upon his death in 1970. No, it was not about "doing everything in moderation." That has become so tiresome. It wasn't that you should treat people as you'd want to be treated yourself either. I would never be so presumptuous. No, it was far better than those old bromides.

Uncle Robb had been talking with one of the young women in our circulation department, the daughter of an old family friend, for a half hour or so at our office in Dublin, New Hampshire. I sat across the room from him in those days and could catch snatches of the conversation. Particularly if my ears were out on stems. Which they were.

It was apparent they were discussing a certain local dandy she'd been seeing — a fellow who had a reputation for getting into fights at the bars over in Brattleboro, Vermont, breaking ladies' hearts at the drop of a hat, and all that sort of thing. Uncle Robb was advising her to drop him. She was crying and saying she cared for him. When she finally left, it didn't seem to me that Uncle Robb had made much headway. In fact, she sounded more determined than ever that, despite his urgings to the contrary, this particular dandy don was the man for her.

Uncle Robb sat quietly for a few minutes, staring out at the pear tree next to his window. Then he got up slowly and ambled over to my desk. I looked up at him standing there in front of me, all six feet four inches of him, and pretended I'd just noticed his presence. It was then he came forth with what I now believe to be the best advice I've ever received.

"Don't ever give advice," he said solemnly. I nodded, waiting for more. I wasn't disappointed. "Unless," he said, after a long, thoughtful pause, "unless you can somehow determine what advice the person wants to hear. Then give that."

In the ensuing years, I've learned a lot about advice and advice giving because that's what *The Old Farmer's Almanac* does every year. Aside, that is, from presenting the astronomical structure for each day — moon and sun risings and settings, tides, and so on — and aside from the monthly weather forecasts for all of North America and aside from maybe a little history based on that year's particular anniversaries. Aside from those areas, it can be truly said that the Almanac has been an annual book of advice ever since 1792, when the first edition appeared on the American scene.

Right from the beginning, the Almanac advised its readers — whether they were farmers or not — on everything from the best times for planting peas and catching the most fish to when to castrate bulls. It has had advice for lovers, advice for curing sickness and staying healthy, advice for making money, advice for restoring energy, advice for proper social behavior, and on and on year after year.

In reading over the past 203 editions specifically for this book, I became aware early on that all Almanac advice seemed, at least to me, to fall into the ten general categories represented by the following ten chapters. Oh, sure, someone might accuse me of stretching a little here and there. For instance, maybe the article in Chapter 3 on whether clams are truly happy has little specific connection with a person's dining room. I have, however, found it to be a topic that can momentarily liven up an otherwise dull conversation around the dining table.

Similarly, one might ask why an article on famous last words appears in the chapter having to do with the room in the house we used to call the parlor. Well, as many older Almanac readers know, the parlor was the room in which you were christened, married — and laid out for final public view.

I would have one piece of personal advice for anyone about to read this book: Please don't attempt to read it cover to cover in, say, one weekend. Instead, peruse it from time to time, choosing the sort of advice you're in the mood for on a particular day. Like the Almanac itself, this is a book for reading in ten- or fifteen-minute segments over a period of twelve months. After all, one can digest only so much advice in one sitting. Perhaps even in one life.

Incidentally, the young woman to whom Uncle Robb was giving advice that day in our office soon married the dandy don. He gave up his wicked ways and became a deacon of the church, and the couple proceeded to raise three lovely children. At this writing, they are still in the process of living happily ever after. As Uncle Robb said himself later on, he should have taken the advice he gave to me that day. But then, that wasn't the sort of advice he really wanted to hear. ✸

PART ONE

Advice for Your Home

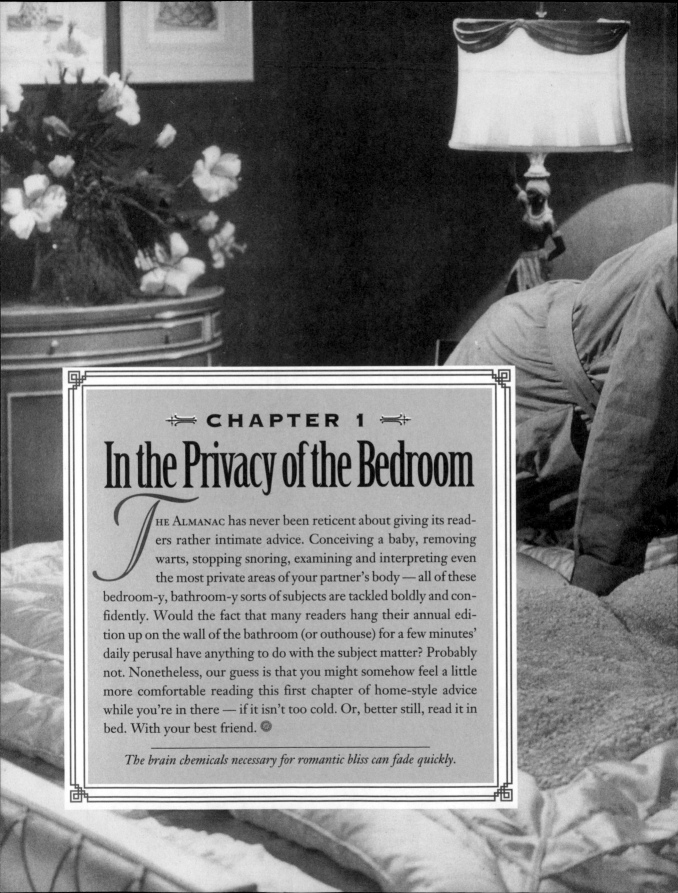

CHAPTER 1
In the Privacy of the Bedroom

THE ALMANAC has never been reticent about giving its readers rather intimate advice. Conceiving a baby, removing warts, stopping snoring, examining and interpreting even the most private areas of your partner's body — all of these bedroom-y, bathroom-y sorts of subjects are tackled boldly and confidently. Would the fact that many readers hang their annual edition up on the wall of the bathroom (or outhouse) for a few minutes' daily perusal have anything to do with the subject matter? Probably not. Nonetheless, our guess is that you might somehow feel a little more comfortable reading this first chapter of home-style advice while you're in there — if it isn't too cold. Or, better still, read it in bed. With your best friend. ✹

The brain chemicals necessary for romantic bliss can fade quickly.

Solving the Mysteries of Love (& Sex)

You might want to take notes while you read the following. It contains not only plenty of good advice (don't, for instance, take your lover to the bedroom after a heavy meal) but also some rather startling information . . .

By Christine Schultz

A S SOON AS SHE SAW his photo in a catalog, she fell in love. All the other merchandise — the corsets, the garters, the studded dog collars — paled in comparison. "I am a lonely schoolteacher in the dismal hills of Idaho," she wrote to the catalog publisher. "Would you be kind enough to do your share in assisting a poor, forlorn teacher in her future happiness by sending this man advertised in your latest edition?"

Americans rate Rhett Butler and Scarlett O'Hara's kiss in Gone with the Wind *as the most memorable in movie history. Here, in anticipation of same, the two are engaged in "The Gaze" — which, scientists say, "triggers a primitive part of the human brain."*

Hers was a classic case of love at first sight, and though seemingly far-fetched, not one to be quickly discounted. As the philosopher Blaise Pascal once said, "The heart has its reasons which reason knows nothing of." Poets for centuries have agreed that the one certainty about love is its mystery. Today's scholars, however, armed with their studies and statistics, aren't so ready to concede. With clipboards in hand, they've taken notes on everything from the flirting sequence gesture to the copulatory gaze to the effects of diet on the libido and the "love drug" on mice. Although they have yet to crack the code, they've discovered some revealing clues about love. Our lonely Idaho schoolmistress would do well to take notes. Perhaps you would, too.

For starters, you should know that if you're a romantic, you're not alone. Scholars have mistakenly believed for too long that courtly love is a luxury invented by the twelfth-century troubadours in Provence and handed down

Brush the hair at least twice weekly and shampoo once a month.

– 1914 –

to us through Western culture. Recently, they've learned (or admitted) that romantic love is, in fact, universal. Of 166 cultures surveyed by anthropologists William Jankowiak and Edward Fischer, some 89 percent showed signs of romantic love. (It's true that many cultures still don't believe romantic love should be the basis of marriage, but the tide is shifting in the heart's favor.) That means you could stumble onto romance almost anywhere — in the Australian outback, in the Amazon jungle, or even in the hills of Idaho.

You may wonder, nevertheless, what exactly to look for in a mate. Try measuring forearms. One study showed that men and women with the same size forearms were more likely to stay together. But if you

At the time of the first kiss, or perhaps even before, neuron messengers from his brain have keyed in to the subtle scent being released from her apocrine glands.

forget your tape measure, the poets say not to worry — you'll know love when you see it: "Through the eyes love attains the heart:/For the eyes are the scouts of the heart" (Guiraud de Borneil). Surprisingly, some scientists agree that you should go with your instincts, since love at first sight most likely evolved to spur the mating process. "During the mating season, a female squirrel needs to breed," explains anthropologist Helen Fisher. "It is not to her advantage to copulate with a porcupine. But if she sees a healthy squirrel, she should waste no time." For squirrels and humans alike, the key attraction lies in the health of the potential mate. Scholars tell us that despite all the worldwide variations, the one physical characteristic that attracts men and women in every culture is a good complexion. (Now, about that blemish . . .)

But it's not just how you look; it's how you smell. Foul odors do little to induce affection. Here's why: Located in our nasal cavities are five million olfactory neurons waiting like postal workers to sort through some ten thousand recognizable odors. They mail these perfumed messages directly to the brain's emotional headquarters (what scientists call the limbic system).

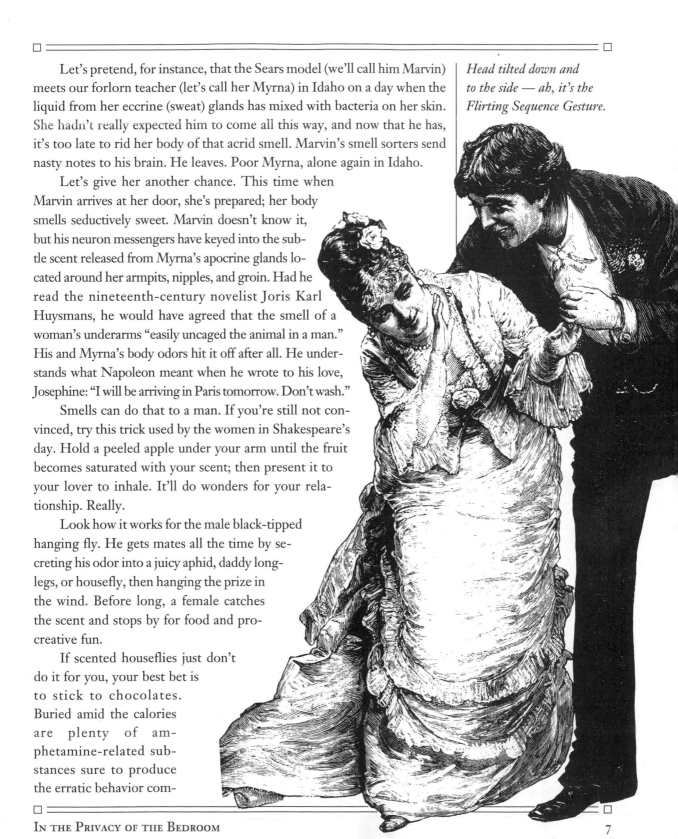

Let's pretend, for instance, that the Sears model (we'll call him Marvin) meets our forlorn teacher (let's call her Myrna) in Idaho on a day when the liquid from her eccrine (sweat) glands has mixed with bacteria on her skin. She hadn't really expected him to come all this way, and now that he has, it's too late to rid her body of that acrid smell. Marvin's smell sorters send nasty notes to his brain. He leaves. Poor Myrna, alone again in Idaho.

Let's give her another chance. This time when Marvin arrives at her door, she's prepared; her body smells seductively sweet. Marvin doesn't know it, but his neuron messengers have keyed into the subtle scent released from Myrna's apocrine glands located around her armpits, nipples, and groin. Had he read the nineteenth-century novelist Joris Karl Huysmans, he would have agreed that the smell of a woman's underarms "easily uncaged the animal in a man." His and Myrna's body odors hit it off after all. He understands what Napoleon meant when he wrote to his love, Josephine: "I will be arriving in Paris tomorrow. Don't wash."

Smells can do that to a man. If you're still not convinced, try this trick used by the women in Shakespeare's day. Hold a peeled apple under your arm until the fruit becomes saturated with your scent; then present it to your lover to inhale. It'll do wonders for your relationship. Really.

Look how it works for the male black-tipped hanging fly. He gets mates all the time by secreting his odor into a juicy aphid, daddy longlegs, or housefly, then hanging the prize in the wind. Before long, a female catches the scent and stops by for food and procreative fun.

If scented houseflies just don't do it for you, your best bet is to stick to chocolates. Buried amid the calories are plenty of amphetamine-related substances sure to produce the erratic behavior com-

Head tilted down and to the side — ah, it's the Flirting Sequence Gesture.

The Worst Thing That Can Happen to You in the Bathroom

A true, horrifying story . . .

FOR ALMOST A WEEK one summer, Laurie and Jules Lamothe of Hamilton, Ontario, had noticed the toilet in their twelfth-floor, two-bedroom apartment operating in a rather sluggish fashion. It didn't seem to flush properly. Then, on August 9, 1987, Laurie discovered why. When she looked into the toilet bowl, there, toward the bottom but apparently squirming to reach the surface of the water, was the head of what turned out to be a five-foot-long boa constrictor. When Laurie screamed and sounded the alarm in no uncertain terms, the snake retreated into the sewer system to which it had escaped from a neighboring apartment a week earlier.

During the following few days, members of the Hamilton Society for the Prevention of Cruelty to Animals (SPCA) attempted to capture the elusive boa by putting dead rats and a guinea pig into the Lamothe toilet bowl, all to no avail. The rescue attempt ended on August 12 when a plumber found a blockage in one of the sewer pipes directly below the Lamothe apartment. The blockage was the boa, which had suffocated to death.

Says Laurie Lamothe, "From now on, I'll always be playing peekaboo with the toilet seat."

Courtesy of Nora Underwood and Maclean's *magazine.*

Editor's note: So that all Almanac readers (and editors) won't also be playing toilet peekaboo from now on, it should be noted that SPCA officials stated that this was the first time they'd ever encountered a boa constrictor caught in a drainpipe. Ever. (But if it can happen once . . .)

mon to infatuation. Food for the heart.

Who can resist a little courtship feeding, the old evolutionary way for a male to show his prowess as a hunter? To keep in shape for his forays, Marvin should fill up on roughage. Lots of it. That's the advice Dr. Frederick Hollick gave back in the 1840s. "To ward off impotence," he counseled, "fill up on potatoes, celery, parsnips, onions, mushrooms, truffles if you can get them, olives, tomatoes, lima beans, and above all, asparagus. Canvasback duck also makes a potent pepper-upper." Those who need self-restraint, on the other hand, should avoid those foods and eschew coffee, particularly, the good doctor said, if they are "disposed to involuntary emissions." In all cases, he advised that lovers would do well to avoid constipation and to take care to let the stomach settle before proceeding to the bedroom. "Sexual indulgence just after eating is nearly certain to be followed by indigestion, even if it does not cause immediate vomiting."

Regrettably, not all in love is savory. If you're serious about finding love, you may wish to sample one of the many concoctions said to ignite the heart (if not the intestines). The Australian aborigines brew a love potion from kangaroo testicles; others swallow the heart of a wild duck; those in the Far East add a bit of ginger to soft drinks, sweets, and tea; the Chinese look to ginseng and rhinoceros horn. If you have trouble finding kangaroo testicles in your local supermarket, you might try a more accessible mixture: stir rosemary, thyme, mint, rose petals, and lemon leaves into black tea. Drink it under a waxing moon.

In fact, almost anything you do concerning love would be better done under the waxing or full moon. Scientists and poets alike agree that the moon has a powerful effect on our reproductive beings. Pliny believed that "lunar energy penetrates all things"; Aristotle noticed that the ovaries of sea urchins swell during the full moon; Darwin wrote that "man is subject, like other mammals, birds, and even insects, to that mysterious law, which causes certain normal processes, such as gestation, as well as the maturation and duration of various diseases to follow lunar periods."

A statistically significant number of births (7 percent) occurs at full moons, and a study by Wesleyan University's psychology department found a 30 percent increase in sexual activity at the time of ovulation, which most frequently happens during the full moon. "Like other mammals that go into heat," writes Paul Katzeff, "women apparently grow randier at ovulation." But they're not the only ones. Researchers have also documented that men, like women, have a greater sexual appetite once a month at the time of the full moon.

For all we know, it could just be the added light that incites us to romance. When the moon doesn't shine, we're left groping in the dark; the darkness signals our pineal glands to produce melatonin, and that puts a damper on sperm production, ovulation, and sexual interest. During a waning moon, you'd be better off waiting for a picnic in the sun. Sunlight raises the excitement level by revving up the pituitary gland and turning on the ovaries and testes.

A recent American study showed that women initiate two-thirds of all sexual liaisons. Their best pickup line goes like this: "Hi." (It works 100 percent of the time.)

Charles Darwin was certain the moon had an effect on gestation; today many scientists agree.

With all these cosmic forces at play on our bodies, do our brains have any say at all in the matter of love?

"If only one could tell true love from false love," said Katherine Mansfield, "as one can tell mushrooms from toadstools." But even that's not such an easy thing. If you're no mycologist, take a quick lesson in body cues. The most obvious, of course, is the human "upper smile," combined with a one-sixtieth-of-a-second eyebrow lift; it's a worldwide indicator of interest. Don't, however, confuse the upper smile with the "nervous social smile." If Marvin, for instance, approaches Myrna with his lips pulled back to reveal his upper *and lower* teeth, Myrna should spot the response as one that evolved from the ancient mammalian practice of baring one's teeth when cornered. Myrna should back off.

She might try to relax Marvin with the Flirting Sequence Gesture, an age-old female courtship ploy diagrammed by ethologist Irenaus Eibl-Eibesfeldt like this: The woman smiles at her admirer, lifting her eyebrows in a swift, jerky motion as she opens her eyes wide. Then she drops her eyelids, tilts her head down and to the side, and looks away. Often she will also cover her face with her hands and giggle nervously.

Marvin may now be impressed. He may wonder, though, why he wasn't the one to initiate such advances. Perhaps he hasn't heard of a study by Clellan Ford and Frank Beach in the 1950s showing that in practice women around the world initiate sexual liaisons. He also might not have heard of another study showing that American women initiated two-thirds of their encounters with men. Their best pickup line went like this: "Hi." It worked 100 percent of the time. Men had only a 71 percent success rate with that same line. But at least it means the ball's rolling.

To keep it moving, watch for the next cue. If a woman turns her toes inward, that's the meekness stance, signaling openness for approach. If the

(continued on page 13)

Taking a Bath Will Help You Live Longer

*Just 2 to 5 quarts of nice, cold water
every day . . .*

EXTEND THE SAME FAVOR, daily, to your whole person, that you do to your face and hands. All you require is two to five quarts of cold water (and as much more as you please) and one or two towels; the whole operation need not occupy five minutes. When you can faithfully and fearlessly wash yourselves all over with cold water daily, you will have taken a vast step in the commencement of uninterrupted health.

The Bath of Diana *(detail), by François Boucher.*

Taking a Bath Can Be One Way to Die

It happens most in Oregon, Nevada, Utah, and Alaska . . .

A S A GENERAL RULE, about one person per day drowns in a bathtub in the United States. The most drownings occur during the spring; the fewest occur during the winter. The fewest drownings per capita take place in New England, Pennsylvania, North Carolina, Tennessee, Mississippi, Louisiana, Iowa, and North Dakota; the most per capita happen in Oregon, Nevada, Utah, and Alaska. (Hot tubs are not included in these statistics.) In 1971, only about one hundred people in the United States drowned in a bathtub, so statistically speaking, taking a bath has become more hazardous.

*Courtesy of Lawrence D. Budnik,
David A. Ross, and the*
American Journal of Public Health.

Early showers were intended to promote "hygienic bathing."

man thrusts out his chest, he's trying to impress. Males throughout the animal kingdom puff themselves up to appear attractive. If these cues click, both male and female are interested, and their eyes lock for two to three seconds, with the pupils dilated. Scientists call this, the most striking human courtship ploy, the Copulatory Gaze. "The gaze triggers a primitive part of the human brain," says anthropologist Helen Fisher, "calling forth one of two basic emotions — approach or retreat."

If neither person backs down, only one thing can happen next: The Kiss. Rhett Butler and Scarlett O'Hara did it best in *Gone with the Wind* — Americans rate that the most memorable kiss in movie history. (Runner-up is the beach kiss by Burt Lancaster and Deborah Kerr in *From Here to Eternity*.) Don't think for a minute that a kiss is just a kiss. On the contrary, it speaks volumes. The esteemed Dr. Bubba Nicholson wrote in the *British Journal of Dermatology* that kissing allows us to taste semiochemicals on a suitor's skin. Semiochemicals, according to Nicholson, transmit biological signals of attraction and compatibility. In the words of Carl Jung, "The meeting of two personalities is like the contact of two chemical substances: if there is any reaction, both are transformed."

So if Marvin and Myrna taste good to each other, they may well fall in love. They may find themselves dizzy with excitement, full of bumbling energy that keeps them up late into the night. They might tell you there's chemistry between them. And it would be true, literally. Michael Liebowitz of the New York State Psychiatric Institute says that during infatuation, the brain releases a chemical called phenylethylamine, or PEA, a natural amphetamine. When scientists inject PEA into mice, the animals jump and squeal, exhibiting "popcorn behavior."

But extended romantic bliss may become too much for the brains of Marvin and Myrna. Liebowitz tells us that eighteen months is about all the brain can take in this revved-up state. Then the nerve endings become habituated to the stimulants, and PEA levels drop. A new set of brain chemicals called endorphins takes over. Endorphins calm the mind, kill pain, and reduce anxiety, leaving Myrna and Marvin comfortably settled in the attachment stage of love. Now they can talk, eat, and sleep in peace. Myrna may discover for the first time that Marvin snores. Loudly. She read somewhere that after sexual intercourse, male rats emit a contented high-frequency snore. Twenty-two kilohertz wouldn't be so bad. At least it wouldn't keep her awake like this jackhammer noise Marvin makes. Since she can't sleep, maybe she'll just go downstairs, do some reading, and flip through a couple of catalogs to see what they have in stock. ✸

For bad breath, swallow half a teaspoon of powdered charcoal in a little cold water.

– 1912 –

Examine Your Bed Partner Very Carefully to Ascertain Character

Today, the following is considered by most (but not all) to be untrustworthy and certainly unscientific. Not so in the eighteenth and nineteenth centuries . . .

EYEBROWS

Eyebrows disclose how a person *reacts* to the world.

- **High brows:** Reserved, aloof, loyal, giving the appearance of shyness.
- **Low brows:** Easygoing, doesn't enjoy thinking.
- **Drooping brows** (toward the temple): Good-natured, optimistic, lacking confidence and vitality.

EYE SHAPE

Each eye is connected to the opposite hemisphere of the brain. The left eye expresses internal feelings; the right eye represents the more outgoing side of a person. As a result, a person's left eye can show suspicion at the same time the right shows friendliness.

- **Narrow eyes:** Selective perception.
- **Wide eyes:** A broad view of life.
- **Visible eyelids:** A doer.
- **No lids show:** Analytic.
- **Bulging eyes:** Extroverted, possessing high self-esteem, incapable of keeping a secret, know-it-all, warm, clever.

- **Deep-set eyes:** Introverted, good adviser, low self-esteem, apathetic.
- **Whites show above and below the eye:** Diabolical, brittle.
- **Wide-set eyes:** Broad perspective, tolerant, with low vitality.

EARS

Ears reflect the way a person *hears* the world.

- **Ears close to the face:** Relates to the present, avoids changes, passive, holds grudges.
- **Ears toward the back of the head:** Future oriented, possessing a healthy ego, aggressive.
- **High ears:** Realistic.
- **Low ears:** Visionary, gets upset when things go wrong, mediocre.
- **Large ears:** Gets the big picture, generous.
- **Very large ears:** Excitable, likable, stubborn, shallow.
- **Small ears:** Hard working, conformist, lacking self-confidence, limited perspective, easily influenced.
- **Tiny ears:** Shrewd, deceitful, prone to violence.

NOSE

The nose relates to power and sex.

- **Average placement of nose:** Enjoys possessions and uses them well.
- **High placement of nose:** Likes solitude.
- **Low nose:** Easygoing.
- **Long nose:** Conservative, achiever, stubborn.
- **Short nose:** Open minded, optimistic, enthusiastic.
- **Large nose:** Aggressive, seeking power.
- **Small nose:** Sensitive, timid, reactive.

CHEEKBONES

- **High bones:** Self-reliant, fighter, power seeker.
- **Low bones:** Exactly the opposite.
- **Prominent bones:** Critical, very demanding.
- **Flat bones:** Easygoing, flexible, avoiding power.

MOUTH & LIPS

The lips and mouth — not only the natural shapes but also what people do to reshape their lips — are giveaways to personality.

- **Full, well-rounded, balanced mouth:** Warm, well integrated, vital, sensitive, sensuous.
- **Wide mouth:** Needs affection, too easygoing, very impetuous.
- **Small mouth:** Reserved, introverted, with low vitality.
- **Thick lips:** Pleasure seeking, warm.
- **Thick lower lip:** Entertaining, appealing, selfish.
- **Thick upper lip:** Verbose, impulsive, could be a liar.
- **Compressed lips:** Rigid.
- **Thin lips:** Precise, withholding, conservative. ✺

NOW WHAT WOULD **YOU** DO IN A CASE LIKE THIS?

"Turn Over, Dear, for God's Sake, Turn Over!"

Snoring levels up to 90 decibels—equivalent to a pneumatic jackhammer—have been recorded, and an estimated 50 million Americans snore. So . . . can anything be done?

By Jim Collins

*T*IS SAID THAT SNORING is the only human frailty that bothers the subject not at all; it merely makes life miserable for those who are forced to endure it. True enough. But one night legendary Texas gunfighter John Wesley Hardin made life miserable for the fellow snoring in the adjacent hotel room. He shot a bullet through the wall and killed the snorer in his sleep.

If the incident is isolated (it isn't unique; in December 1983, a Dallas woman calmly pulled a gun from beneath the covers and fired five shots into her bedmate, who "snored too loudly"), at least the motive behind such a violent reaction is familiar to many. Countless hours of sleep have been lost over the years in army barracks, dormitories, and bedrooms, causing severe embarrassment, ruining hunting trips, straining relationships, and worse. A 1971 issue of *Eye, Ear, Nose, and Throat Monthly* reported that snoring had finally been declared legal grounds for divorce.

Chuckle if you will. Snorers have long been the stuff of humor, from Charles Dickens's character Joe in *The Pickwick Papers* to memorable scenes by Zero Mostel and The Three Stooges. Over in the medical community, however, no one is laughing. In addition to its social implications, snoring has been linked with elevated blood pressure, cardiovascular stress, headaches, depression, excessive sleepiness, and fatigue. Behind alcohol, excessive sleepiness is the second leading cause of highway fatalities, and fatigue costs American industry an estimated $70 billion each year in lowered productivity and avoidable accidents.

Till ere the splendid visions close
We snore quartettes of ecstasy in nose.
— Samuel Taylor Coleridge, 1790

WHO SNORES THE MOST?

As the old adage goes, "Laugh and the world laughs with you. Snore and you sleep alone." True, but if you do snore, you aren't alone in your isolation. An estimated fifty million Americans are afflicted with the ailment. And you certainly aren't in poor company. Twenty of the first thirty-two U.S. presidents were known to snore, including Washington, Lincoln, both Adamses, both Roosevelts, Taft, Hoover, and Grant. So were Mussolini (he was renowned), Hemingway, Lord Chesterfield, and even Beau Brummell, the ladies' man.

What do these men have in common? A rogues' gallery of famous snorers (clockwise from upper left): Beau Brummell, Benito Mussolini, Ernest Hemingway, and John Quincy Adams.

How to Fall Asleep Quickly
(1854)

How to get to sleep is, to many persons, a matter of high importance. Nervous persons, who are troubled with wakefulness and excitability, usually have a strong tendency of blood to the brain, with cold extremities. The pressure of blood on the brain keeps it in a stimulated or wakeful state, and the pulsations in the head are often painful.

Let such rise and chafe the body and extremities with a harsh towel, or rub smartly with the hands, to promote circulation, and withdraw the excessive amount of blood from the brain, and they will fall asleep in a few moments. A cold bath, or sponge bath, and rubbing, or a good run, or rapid walk in the open air, or going up and down stairs a few times, just before retiring, will aid in equalizing circulation and promoting sleep.

These rules are simple and easy of application in castle or cabin, and may minister to the comfort of thousands who would freely expend money for an anodyne to promote "Nature's sweet restorer — balmy sleep."

Between the ages of twenty and thirty-five, 20 percent of all American men and 5 percent of all American women snore; by age sixty the percentages rise to 60 and 40, respectively. These statistics don't lie. Men are much more likely to snore than women; old people more likely than young. So there's a good chance you're either already snoring or you will be in the near future. Or somebody close to you does or will. What, then, is there to do?

EXACTLY WHY WE SNORE

Snoring, very simply, is caused by the vibrations of the soft tissues at the back of the throat. The sounds originate from restricted air flowing through the collapsible part of the airway—roughly from the epiglottis to the choanae—where there is no rigid support. The seriousness of the snoring depends entirely on how restricted that airway is.

In general, three factors contribute to the bad vibrations: weak or inadequate musculature, space-occupying masses encroaching on the airway, and obstructed nasal breathing. Different factors influence people to different degrees, sometimes alone and sometimes in combination.

The first factor explains why most snoring occurs during the deep stages of sleep, when the muscles in the back of the throat relax, lose their tone, and even fold into each other. The relaxed, limp muscles of the upper throat descend into the airway, and the tongue falls back, causing vibrations. Understanding gravity, it's easy to see why snoring often occurs when people sleep on their backs. Understanding aging, it's easy to see how less active, more sedentary people are often afflicted. And since the aging process tends to have a greater impact on men's muscle tone than on women's (men simply have more mass that can atrophy), it's easy to start understanding why men are the more common snorers. There's no truth, then, to the old husbands' tale that primitive men snored to protect their women, their noises frightening away the nightly beasts of prey.

The second factor — things that take up room in the vicinity of the airway — can sometimes be blamed on heredity. In children, for instance, snoring can almost always be traced to enlarged tonsils and adenoids. And although the average-size uvula (that fleshy, lobe-shaped thing that hangs down in the back of your throat) measures a quarter inch, some poor souls have one that's closer to four times that. Inherited traits can be exacerbated, too.

In 1897, one S. Anderson invented this mouthpiece for the prevention of snoring.

Obese people are three times more likely to snore than thin ones (their bulkiness and lack of muscle tone extend throughout their bodies, not just the visible parts). Smokers irritate their pharynxes daily, causing the mucous membranes to swell, narrowing the airway. So if you had to guess who snores and you picked a large, sedentary, male smoker — say, Orson Welles, just to pick a name (he was a first-class snorer) — you'd probably be right.

The third factor involves obstructed or irregular nasal breathing. Congestion, hay fever, polyps, even a deviated septum from your old boxing days can be the culprit, creating negative pressure during inspiration, which in turn draws together the soft tissues of the collapsible airway. Which in turn causes snoring.

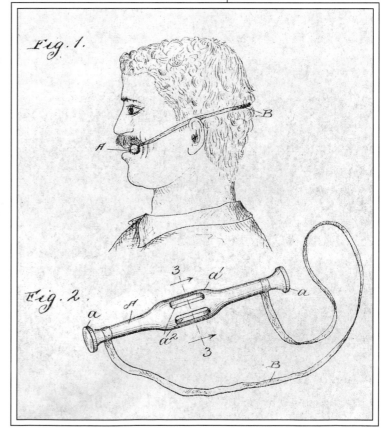

During the most advanced stage of snoring, the passage becomes completely blocked. The sleeper actually stops breathing for a period before he or she is jolted awake — which causes the relaxed muscles to tighten and reopen the airway. Labored breathing may continue for a while before the process is repeated, then repeated again, often accompanied by gasping, choking, and violent body spasms — all symptoms of a condition known as obstructed sleep apnea (from the Greek *apnoea*, "want of breath"). The social fallout of the problem is obvious, but it's nothing compared with the more serious dangers: apnea has led to severe behavioral, cardiac, and pulmonary problems, and in several instances sleep apnea has resulted in cardiac arrest and death. So much for quartets of ecstasy.

OLD-TIME "CURES"

The most popular cure for snoring, historically, can be traced back to the Revolutionary War, when soldiers sewed a small cannonball into a pocket on the back of a snoring comrade's nightshirt. Variations on this device — intended to discourage the sleeper from sleeping on his back, thus keeping the tongue forward and the airway open — have appeared periodically ever since then. Leonidas Wilson applied for a patent in 1900 on a leather harness that strapped a multipronged object between the wearer's shoulder blades. Other antisnoring devices (there are more than three hundred registered with the U.S. Patent Office, most of them invented by men) include all manner of straitjackets and restraining harnesses based on the same premise. The method of choice today is a pocket sewn on the back of a pajama top, containing (in lieu of a cannonball) a marble, golf ball, or tennis ball. Some creative people have been known to use jacks or bottle caps. The message is the same as a sharp elbow from a companion or a shoe thrown across a bunkroom: turn over.

For many mild or infrequent snorers, these methods are successful, even to the point of conditioning the snorer to abandon sleeping on his or her back. The trouble is, not all snorers are mild or infrequent. Seven out of ten snore just as well on their sides as on their backs.

Other attempts have focused on extending the snorer's neck or jaw to help keep the airway open, as in Cyrus Johnson's mouth-restraining device patented in 1948 or the ground-breaking experiments of St. Louis physician Robert Elman in the early 1960s. A more common approach has been to force the snorer's mouth shut — thereby forcing him to breathe through his nose. (Francis Pulford's "facial molding device" did that in 1893, as did John Rothenberger's "anti-mouth breathing device" twenty-six years later.)

> When the hair is inclined to be harsh and dry, a moderate application of bear's grease or other dressing should be used.
>
> – 1873 –

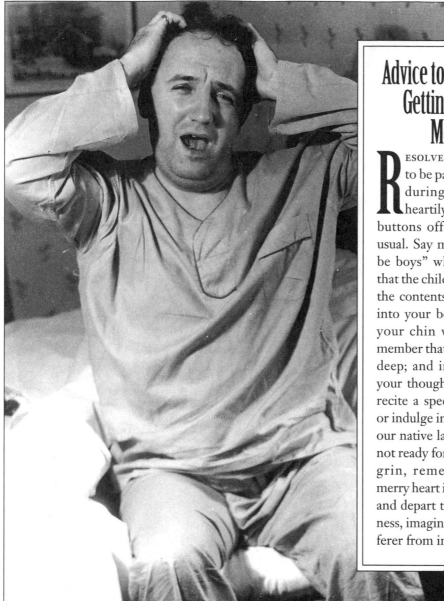

Advice to Husbands on Getting Up in the Morning

RESOLVE IN THE MORNING to be patient and cheerful during the day. Laugh heartily on finding all the buttons off your shirt — as usual. Say merrily, "Boys will be boys" when you discover that the children have emptied the contents of the water jug into your boots. On gashing your chin with a razor, remember that beauty is but skin deep; and in order to divert your thoughts from the pain, recite a speech from *Hamlet*, or indulge in the harmonies of our native land. If breakfast is not ready for you, chuckle and grin, remembering that a merry heart is a continual feast, and depart to your daily business, imagining yourself a sufferer from indigestion.

Apparently, proponents of this method overlook the possibility of the nose being obstructed at the same time, leaving the snorer no way to breathe at all. Or maybe they don't overlook that possibility. . . .

Still other devices have come and gone and come again. Nasal tubes. Neck collars. Chin straps. Respirators. Even sophisticated electronic gadgets that deliver shocks or other startling stimuli to patients when they snore. Mail-order catalogs are filled with these "guaranteed" cures and "miracle" treatments. "They all work for some people," says Dr. Martin Scharf, director of the Sleep Disorders Center at Cincinnati's Mercy Hospital of Fairfield. "They're all worth a try. But first try nasal spray."

Advice to (Prospective) Wives on Going to Bed at Night

- Cut a lemon in half, rub both halves on the four corners of your bed, and sleep with the lemon halves under your pillow. If you see the one you love in a dream, he or she will be faithful to you. If you don't dream of the one you love, he or she will be unfaithful.
- Swallow nine pills made of grated hazelnut, walnut, and nutmeg, plus butter and sugar. You will dream of your perfect mate's occupation.
- Eat a thimbleful of salt before going to bed. The one who brings you water in your dreams will be your lover.

WHAT YOU SHOULD DO NOW

Taking Dr. Scharf's approach, try these:

1. Reduce your weight and tone your muscles. Better eating habits and general exercise will help firm up the flaccid throat tissues causing so much noise.

2. Better still, perform prescribed "mouth exercises" to isolate the particular jaw and throat muscles that affect the airway. Learn some from your local sleep disorders clinic.

3. Avoid eating large meals or taking depressants or muscle relaxants before going to bed. This includes alcohol, warm milk, antihistamines, and, ironically, sleeping pills. Take instead prescription medications that clear nasal passages, stimulate respiration, or promote wakefulness.

4. Sleep on a firm mattress with a single pillow in a cool, well-ventilated room. Don't use a large pillow or pillows that force you to bend at the waist or neck (which puts pressure on the diaphragm and abdomen). Tilting the entire bed by placing bricks below the bedposts at the head of the bed will help relieve pressure in those same areas and drain congested nasal passages.

5. Consult your allergist — your solution may be as simple as replacing a feather pillow with a synthetic one.

6. Quit smoking.

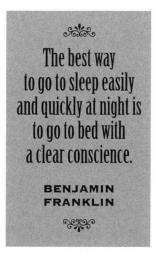

The best way
to go to sleep easily
and quickly at night is
to go to bed with
a clear conscience.

**BENJAMIN
FRANKLIN**

THERE ARE, of course, more drastic solutions. Orthodontic appliances can be fitted. Machines providing "continuous, positive airway pressure" can be prescribed. Routine surgery can remove polyps or straighten septums. Other surgery can trim away some of the excess tissue in the throat cavity, enlarging the airway. (The procedure is uvulo-palato-pharyngoplasty, but you might want to refer to it as UPPP when you inquire about it.) And there are medications that might work in your particular situation. The best advice? Consult your family physician or an ear, nose, and throat specialist, especially if you suspect you suffer from apnea. You'll sleep better for it. And so will your spouse.

A final thought. Snoring levels up to ninety decibels have been recorded in the lab — equivalent to a pneumatic jackhammer blasting concrete. (The deep-throated diesel sounds from the back of a Greyhound bus are closer to forty.) Winston Churchill was said to be a thirty-five-decibel man, although he didn't come close to Canadian Mark Thompson Hebbard, the current world record holder. On November 3, 1987, Hebbard hit a peak of ninety decibels in Vancouver, British Columbia. A Vancouver city bylaw stipulates a maximum of eighty decibels for acceptable traffic noise. ●

How to Have a Baby

Anyone with the brains of a bunny can raise a happy, healthy, successful child by following a few simple rules.

By Tim Clark

L ET'S FACE IT, these are tough times to have a baby. There are so many authorities offering so much conflicting advice on how to raise children. Fortunately, people have managed to do it for thousands of years, even without Japanese-language flash cards or crib mobiles that teach particle physics. The following bits of folk wisdom have been collected from all over the United States and will help anxious parents to determine the sex of the child, care for the baby, and predict his or her future career.

CONCEPTION

- A couple who go to a picture show within three days of getting married will have twins.
- If you dream of your mother giving birth, you will soon have a child.
- If a woman lays her hat or coat on a strange bed, she will have a child.
- Give away old baby clothes, and you'll soon need them again.
- If a woman leaves a diaper under a bed in another's house, a baby will soon be born in that house.

- Attach your wedding ring to a string and dangle it inside a glass tumbler, asking, "How many children shall I have?" Count the number of times the ring strikes the side of the glass, and you will have your answer.
- Holding a child on your first visit to the mother will help you conceive.

BOY OR GIRL?

- To have a boy, a woman should hold a nickel in her mouth at the time of conception.

- A baby conceived in the light of the moon (from new moon to full moon) will be a boy.
- A baby conceived in the dark of the moon (full moon to new moon) will be a girl.
- If the woman has no morning sickness, she is carrying a boy.
- If her stomach comes to a point, she is to have a girl.
- Add the mother's age at conception to the number of the month of conception. If it is even, a girl will be born. If odd, it'll be a boy.
- If the mother eats grapefruit just before conceiving, the child will be a girl.
- If the mother eats vinegar just before conceiving, it will be a boy.
- A baby carried high is a boy; low, a girl.
- During the last three months of pregnancy, count the baby's heartbeats. If they range from 120 to 140 beats per minute, it's a boy; from 140 to 160 beats, it's a girl.
- If the father is sick during the first three months of pregnancy, the child will be male.
- If the mother sleeps with her right hand under her head during pregnancy, she will have a girl. If she sleeps with her left hand under her head, she'll have a boy.

- If the mother craves sweets during pregnancy, her child will be female. If she craves sour things, the child will be male.

AT BIRTH

- Labor pains can be eased by putting an ax under the bed.
- If a laboring woman wears her husband's hat, her pain will be lessened.

- A woman frightened by fire during pregnancy will have a red-haired child.
- Heartburn during pregnancy signifies a child with a lot of hair.

PERSONALITY

- The child will grow up with a disposition just like that of the first person who takes her outdoors.

LOOKS

- Pretty babies become ugly adults and vice versa.
- Call a child "Piggy" to make her grow.
- To make a child grow tall, put manure inside his shoes.
- To make a child grow faster, sweep his feet with a broom.
- Washing babies in urine makes them handsome.

- If the baby's fists are tightly clenched at birth, he will be stingy.
- A baby who cries during baptism likes her name.
- March babies make fickle adults.
- A child born in the light of the moon will be intelligent.
- A child born on a stormy night will be nervous.

- A baby born with a cowlick will be stubborn; a baby with two cowlicks will bright.
- A baby who never falls out of bed during the first year will grow up to be a fool.
- Feed the baby right out of

the pot or skillet, and the child will never run away from home.

PROSPECTS
- On your first visit to a new baby, kiss the soles of her feet for luck.
- Carry a new baby upstairs before going downstairs so that he will rise in the world. If born on the top floor, hold his head near the ceiling.
- Don't take the baby downhill on her first trip away from home. Her fortunes will sink.
- Rub the baby's tongue with a slice of apple immediately after birth, and he will have a good singing voice.
- Crack the first louse you find in your baby's hair on a Bible, and the child will become a preacher.
- A child born foot foremost can't be kept in jail.
- A child born with a caul will be able to tell fortunes.
- A baby born with teeth will suffer ill luck.
- A baby born on the twenty-sixth of the month will get rich.
- The child will grow up to be wealthy if the initials of her full name spell a word.
- A child born around four o'clock in the afternoon will get rich.
- A child born on Christmas Day can understand the speech of animals.

SICKNESS & HEALTH
- Burn the first dirty diaper, and the child will have no stomachaches.
- If the child is croupy, mix a lock of her hair with the mortar in a new house.
- For croup, feed the baby jaybird soup.
- Lay a grunting child in the pigpen to make him stop.
- After feeding a baby, let a puppy lick the child's face. This will prevent illness.

THINGS TO AVOID
- The first time you dress your baby, use old clothes. New clothes will bring bad luck.
- Rain falling on a child's face before her first birthday will cause freckles.
- Frightening a baby will make him knock-kneed.
- Cutting a baby's toenails in the first year of life will cause the child to become pigeon-toed.
- Putting a baby on an ironing board is bad luck.

LEARNING TO WALK
- Set the baby behind the front door for nine mornings, and she will learn to walk sooner.
- If the baby is slow to walk, bury him naked in earth up to his waist with a string tied around his ankle.
- Run up and down stairs with an infant to make her spry.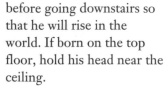

Another Sure-Fire (?) Formula
for Conceiving a Boy or a Girl
(CIRCA 1850)

WHEN IT IS DESIRED to bless the household with a male child, the husband should take good substantial food and moderate exercise, pass his time pleasantly in the gay society of women, read amusing books, and abstain from cohabitation for a time previous to the procreative period. During the same time, the expectant mother should live sparingly, particularly on vegetables, fatigue herself every day, and pass her time in the dry society of old women.

To have female children, the opposite should be observed: the woman should partake freely of stimulating food, using spices freely, but should restrain any passion she might have and preserve its whole force for the desired time. The man, on the contrary, should reduce his physical abilities by actual physical labor and, at the same time, reduce his procreative propensities by frequent, copious cold ablutions.

Courtesy of Dorothy Murray.

A Sampling of Advice on Certain Private Problems

Such as getting rid of warts, falling in love, restoring one's manhood, dealing with freckles, and curing earaches . . .

46 Ways to Make Warts Go Away
By Tim Clark

SIMPLE & EASY

- Buy 5 cents' worth of candy and eat it all.
- Rub the warts seven times with a gold ring.
- Rub with dandelion juice.
- Wash your hands in water used to boil potatoes.
- Count them each night for nine nights.
- Give a pin to a girl who is not related to you.
- Sell the warts to someone, and don't spend the money.
- Rub a wart on St. Abdon's Day (July 30).
- Rub it with the sole of your shoe.
- Point your finger at it and say "Tige" three times.

The Wicked Witch of the West was an expert on warts.

- Rub it with an onion.
- Wish your warts onto a gray horse's backside.
- Cross two pins over a wart, then hide them.
- Wrap a pea in a rag and throw it down a well.
- Give your warts names, and think good things about them.

BIZARRE & COMPLICATED

- Put as many stones as you have warts in a bag. Toss the bag over your right shoulder onto a road. Whoever picks up the bag will get the warts.
- Find a bone, turn it over, and throw it away. Walk off without looking back.
- Cut an apple in half, rub each half over the wart, tie the halves together, and throw them away.
- Rub it with coffee grounds, put the grounds in a bag, and bury the bag.
- Rub it with seven kernels of corn, then feed the corn to your neighbor's chickens.
- Look at the new moon and rub the wart three times, saying "You grow and you go" each time.
- Write a wish on a piece of paper, go to a crossroads, and then tear up the paper and scatter it to the wind.
- Without telling anyone, pick up a stone at midnight,

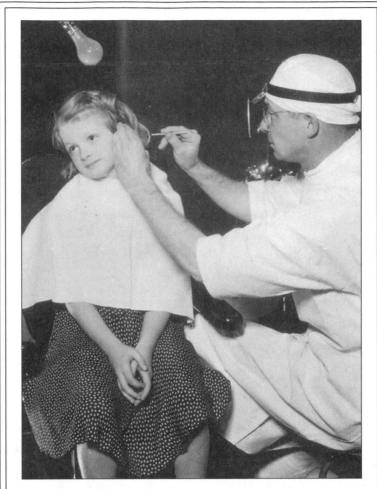

Three Ways to Cure an Earache

- Take a small piece of cotton batting or cotton wool, make a depression in the center with the finger, and then fill it up with as much ground pepper as will rest on a 5-cent piece. Gather it into a ball and tie it up. Dip the ball into sweet oil and insert it in the ear, covering the latter with cotton wool, and use a bandage or cap to retain it in its place. You will experience almost instant relief.
- Roast a piece of lean mutton, squeeze out the juice, and drop the juice into the ear as hot as can be borne.
- Roast an onion and put it into the ear as hot as can be borne.

Courtesy of Brayden Books, Westport, Connecticut.

spit on it, and put it on a rafter in the attic. After eight weeks, turn it over.

FAINTLY REPELLENT

- Prick the wart with a pin; put the blood on a cloth and the cloth in the path of a stranger. If the stranger picks it up, he or she will get the wart.
- Tie a dog's hair very tightly around the wart.
- Rub it with a fish.
- Make the wart bleed, smear the blood on a bean leaf,

hide the leaf under a stone, and walk away backward.

- Wait until someone dies, then go to the graveyard at midnight and call to the devil. He will take your warts away.
- Kiss the wart, then kiss someone else.
- Rub it with a pebble, then toss the pebble into an open grave.
- Rub it with a chicken's foot.
- Rush up and seize the person with the wart, then spit on it.
- Lick the wart when you awaken, before eating or drinking.

EXTREMELY DISGUSTING

- Rub it with cow's urine.

- Rub it with a snail.
- Rub it with chicken intestines.
- Rub it with a rooster's head.
- Cover it with cow manure.
- Mash ants on it.
- Rub it with dirt from a new grave.

DOWNRIGHT CRIMINAL

- Rub stolen meat on it, then bury the meat.
- Steal a dishcloth and hide it.
- Steal a piece of chalk, rub it on the wart, and throw it away.
- Kill a black cat, take it to a graveyard at midnight, and rub it on the wart.
- Wash the wart in the blood of a black cat killed in the light of the moon.
- Rub it with the hand of a corpse. ❇

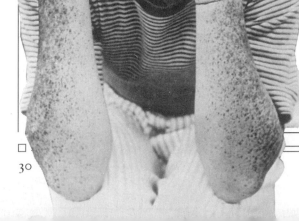

To Take Off Freckles

TAKE BEAN FLOWER water or elder flower water or May dew, gathered from corn, in the quantity of four spoonfuls. Add to it one spoonful of oil of tartar. Mix it well together and often wash the face with it and let it dry on. **(1793)**

OR: Grate a fresh horseradish root very fine, cover with fresh buttermilk, and let stand overnight. Strain through cheesecloth and wash the face morning and night with the resulting liquor. **(1914)**

Harry Shaw of New Jersey, a freckles champ.

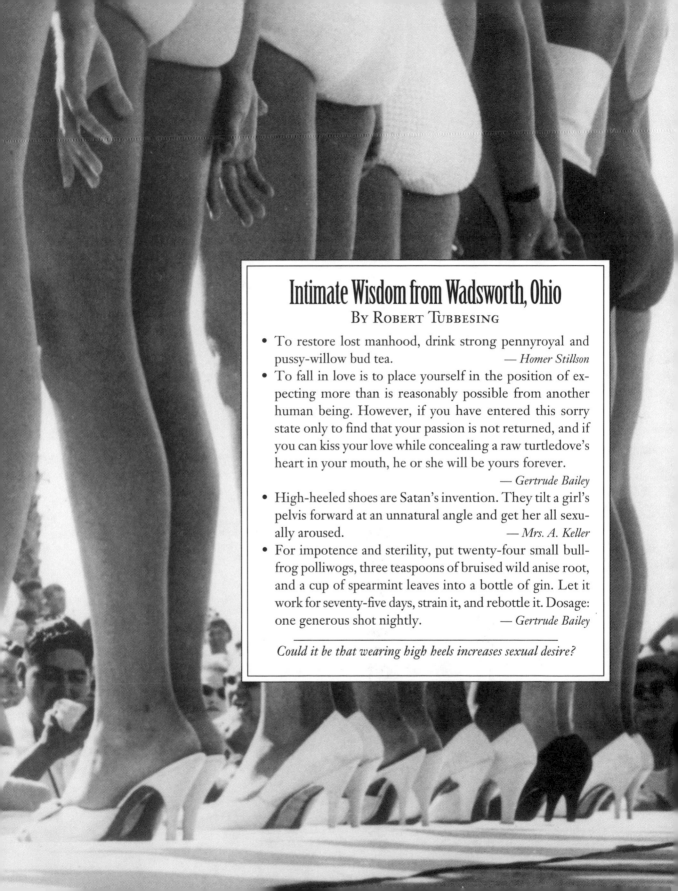

Intimate Wisdom from Wadsworth, Ohio

BY ROBERT TUBBESING

- To restore lost manhood, drink strong pennyroyal and pussy-willow bud tea. — *Homer Stillson*
- To fall in love is to place yourself in the position of expecting more than is reasonably possible from another human being. However, if you have entered this sorry state only to find that your passion is not returned, and if you can kiss your love while concealing a raw turtledove's heart in your mouth, he or she will be yours forever.

    — *Gertrude Bailey*

- High-heeled shoes are Satan's invention. They tilt a girl's pelvis forward at an unnatural angle and get her all sexually aroused. — *Mrs. A. Keller*
- For impotence and sterility, put twenty-four small bullfrog polliwogs, three teaspoons of bruised wild anise root, and a cup of spearmint leaves into a bottle of gin. Let it work for seventy-five days, strain it, and rebottle it. Dosage: one generous shot nightly. — *Gertrude Bailey*

Could it be that wearing high heels increases sexual desire?

≒ CHAPTER 2 ≒

From Soup to the Kitchen Sink

SINCE THE ALMANAC was initially written for farmers rather than farmers' wives, our present-day editorial emphasis on old-fashioned foods and recipes was slow to evolve. In the early days, it was probably assumed that women didn't need any cooking advice — particularly from men, which Almanac editors always were. The only food-related features during the 1790s, for instance, were those such as "The Art of Making Cheese" or "To Refine Sugar." The first specific recipe didn't appear until 1800. After describing "how to roast a piece of beef," it provided instructions for making an onion sauce. ("Put them into a clean sauce-pan with a good piece of butter, a little salt and a gill of sweet cream; stir them over the fire . . .") From then on, food and recipes became more and more an integral part of each year's fare.

The suggestions in this chapter, however, are gleaned from the editions of this century. ✸

In the 1950s, the fully equipped kitchen was a woman's dream.

Praise the Lard & Pass the Flaky Pie Crust

The "forgotten shortening" is making a comeback — and some people, particularly in the Midwest, need no convincing.

By Susan Peery

O NCE UPON A TIME and long ago B.C. (Before Cholesterol), when pigs were plump and pie crusts were short, lard was the fat of choice for many people. Often there was no choice — where butter was dear, manufactured products were nonexistent, and pigs were plentiful, lard was the only shortening used for pastry making, baking, and frying. "Lard bucket" was no term of opprobrium; it simply meant the useful tin pail in which lard was sold and stored.

Lard is a valuable byproduct of hog slaughtering, a no-waste process that allowed frugal farmers to boast that they used everything but the squeal. Lard is made by the simple process of heating, or rendering, the natural hog fat (mostly back fat and "leaf" fat, the internal fat around the abdomen) to separate it from the fine connective tissues (which, after rendering, are known as cracklings). Connective tissue cells hold a plastic mixture of fats much the way a honeycomb holds honey. The melted fat, which turns creamy white when chilled, needs no further refining. It is lard.

During the early years of settlement in the Midwest and Great Plains, pigs were often left outdoors to forage. The skinny, half-wild creatures finally rounded up for slaughter were referred to scornfully as "prairie racers" by one Wisconsin farmer. By 1900, thanks to better husbandry and feed, the average pig was more than 15 percent lard, and production boomed. A hog that dressed out at 165 pounds yielded about 35 pounds of lard and 127 pounds of meat (the squeal apparently accounted for the rest).

Lard met its first serious competition in 1911, when Procter & Gamble patented a hydrogenation process that led to the introduction of Crisco, a solidified vegetable shortening. Although Crisco and its imitators, which can be stored at room temperature without becoming rancid, cut into lard sales, they also provided a point of comparison. Good cooks insisted that lard had better shortening power than other fats, was easily workable over a wide range of temperatures, produced excellent results when used for deep-fat frying, and was more digestible.

During the Great Depression, declining exports of lard (especially to the German market) and desperation slaughtering of hogs by Dust Bowl farmers who couldn't afford to feed glutted the market with lard. The

---

I've never met
a trollop who was
a good cook or
a good cook who was
a trollop.

— 1930 —
MRS. A. KELLER

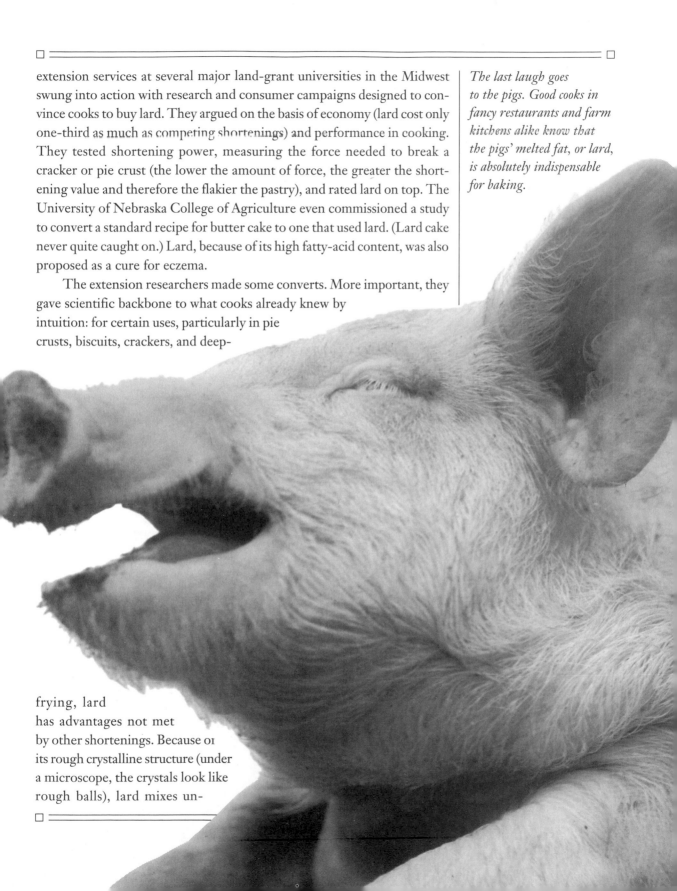

extension services at several major land-grant universities in the Midwest swung into action with research and consumer campaigns designed to convince cooks to buy lard. They argued on the basis of economy (lard cost only one-third as much as competing shortenings) and performance in cooking. They tested shortening power, measuring the force needed to break a cracker or pie crust (the lower the amount of force, the greater the shortening value and therefore the flakier the pastry), and rated lard on top. The University of Nebraska College of Agriculture even commissioned a study to convert a standard recipe for butter cake to one that used lard. (Lard cake never quite caught on.) Lard, because of its high fatty-acid content, was also proposed as a cure for eczema.

The extension researchers made some converts. More important, they gave scientific backbone to what cooks already knew by intuition: for certain uses, particularly in pie crusts, biscuits, crackers, and deep-

The last laugh goes to the pigs. Good cooks in fancy restaurants and farm kitchens alike know that the pigs' melted fat, or lard, is absolutely indispensable for baking.

frying, lard has advantages not met by other shortenings. Because of its rough crystalline structure (under a microscope, the crystals look like rough balls), lard mixes un-

ing a song of sixpence, a pocket full of rye;
Four and twenty Blackbirds baked in a pie.
When the pie was opened, the birds began to sing,
Was not that a dainty dish to set before the King?

Shortening power was often tested by measuring the force needed to break a pie crust. (The lower the force, the flakier the pie crust.)

evenly with flour, leaving unincorporated bits of fat to provide flakiness. (Other shortenings form needlelike crystals that incorporate more smoothly with liquids to create light, even-textured cakes and icings.) In deep-frying, lard imparts an attractive golden crust and may be heated as high as 425°F without smoking.

Although as late as 1978 the National Live Stock and Meat Board in Chicago was promoting lard in its pamphlet *Lard Makes It Better*, the trend since World War II has been away from lard. Let's face it, lard became déclassé. As dietitians urged folks to eat less animal fat, the pork industry worked on breeding hogs down from 15 percent lard to less than 5 percent — back to the prairie racers! The National Pork Producers Council likes to describe pork as white meat (read "low fat") and no longer promotes the use of lard. The council probably wishes we would all forget that lard and pigs have any connection at all.

Some people have never forgotten. Cooks in fancy restaurants and farm kitchens alike know that judicious use of lard in products such as pie crusts and biscuits produces a superior product. Jasper White, chef at the esteemed Boston restaurant Jasper's, makes his pie crusts using shortening in a ratio of two-thirds lard to one-third butter. Diana Kennedy, in her book *The Art of Mexican Cooking* (Bantam, 1989), reports on the extensive use of lard in traditional Mexican cooking and calls lard "absolutely indispensable" for making tamales and in frying beans. "The flavor of homemade lard is incomparable," she writes, "and what's more, you're not getting any preservatives." A Wisconsin grandmother swears by her recipe for cherry cobbler, which uses biscuits made with lard to "cobble" the cherries.

The recipes that follow capitalize on lard's fine shortening power and show its versatility. If you have a favorite biscuit, doughnut, or pie crust recipe using butter or another shortening and you wish to convert it to lard, remember this rule of thumb: use four-fifths as much lard as butter; use only three-fourths as much lard as solid vegetable shortening. Count the calories saved as another plus for lard. Spend those calories on your second piece of pie!

TENDER FLAKY PASTRY

2 cups flour	6 tablespoons ice water
½ teaspoon salt	(approximately)
⅔ cup lard	

Place the flour and salt in a bowl and whisk to blend. Cut in the lard, using a pastry blender, two knives, or your fingers, until the particles are the size of peas. Add ice water 1 tablespoon at a time until the dough just holds together. Form the dough into two balls, one slightly larger than the other, and flatten each to about 1 inch high. Wrap both rounds well in plastic and chill for at least 1 hour. Roll out the rounds on a lightly floured board, using the larger portion for the bottom crust. Do not stretch the dough. Fill as desired.

Makes 1 double crust for an 8- or 9-inch pie.
(The recipe may be halved to make a single pie shell.)

HOMEMADE BISCUIT MIX

8 cups flour	2 teaspoons salt
¼ cup baking powder	1 cup lard

Sift the flour, baking powder, and salt together. Cut the lard into the dry ingredients with a pastry blender until the mixture has a fine, even crumb. Cover and store the dough in the refrigerator until you're ready to use it. This mixture will keep for at least a month. *Makes 10 cups biscuit mix.*

To make biscuits: Preheat the oven to 450°F. Add ½ cup milk to 2 cups Homemade Biscuit Mix and toss until all the ingredients are combined. Turn the mixture out onto a lightly floured surface and knead gently for about 20 seconds. Pat or roll the dough to a ½-inch thickness and cut it with a medium-size (2-inch) biscuit cutter. Bake for 12 to 15 minutes, or until golden. Serve hot.

Makes 10 to 12 biscuits.

During the Depression, farmers slaughtered their hogs when they couldn't buy feed. The resulting lard was heavily advertised, but the market was glutted nonetheless.

N. K. FAIRBANK & CO'S LARD Can be had of any FIRST CLASS Grocer in the UNITED STATES.

FAIRBANK'S REFINERY

PURE LEAF LARD

RED CHERRY COBBLER

1 can (16 ounces) tart red
   cherries
⅓ cup brown sugar
3 tablespoons cornstarch
½ cup orange juice
2 tablespoons butter
⅛ teaspoon salt

½ teaspoon almond extract
1½ cups Homemade Biscuit Mix
   (see earlier recipe)
⅓ cup sugar
¼ teaspoon freshly grated nutmeg
1 egg
¼ cup milk

Preheat the oven to 350°F. Drain the cherries, reserving the juice. Combine the brown sugar and cornstarch in a saucepan. Stir in the cherry juice, orange juice, butter, and salt. Cook, stirring constantly, until the mixture has thickened. Stir in the cherries and almond extract.

For the biscuit topping, combine the Homemade Biscuit Mix, sugar, and nutmeg. Beat the egg and milk together and stir them into the biscuit mixture until combined.

Heat the cherry mixture to boiling, then pour it into a low 1-quart baking dish. Drop the biscuit batter by spoonfuls (about six) on top of the hot cherry mixture. Bake for 35 to 40 minutes, or until the biscuits are golden. Serve warm. *Makes 6 servings.*

SOUR MILK DOUGHNUTS

3½ cups flour
½ teaspoon salt
1 teaspoon baking soda
½ teaspoon baking powder
1 teaspoon freshly grated
   nutmeg
½ teaspoon ginger

¾ cup sugar
2 tablespoons lard
2 eggs
1 cup sour milk or buttermilk
Lard to melt for deep-frying
Sugar for rolling (optional)

Judicious use of lard in products such as pie crusts and biscuits produces superior products.

Sift the dry ingredients (except the sugar) three times. Cream the sugar and lard well, add the eggs, and beat with an electric mixer. Add the milk to the egg mixture and beat well. Add the sifted dry ingredients all at once and mix well. Cover and chill for 1 hour.

Divide the dough into two parts and roll each on a floured board to a ½-inch thickness. Cut the dough with a doughnut cutter. Melt the lard in a deep fryer and heat it to 375°F. Fry the doughnuts quickly, turning them as soon as they come to the top (do not crowd the kettle). Cook the doughnuts until they are golden brown. If desired, roll them in granulated sugar while they are still hot. The lard may be strained, covered, stored in the refrigerator, and used again for frying. *Makes about 2 dozen doughnuts.*

Eating (& Drinking) Right

(1930s)

- **Sometimes I'll bury an oak cask full of my distillings in the manure pile.** It ages three times as fast this way as the ordinary way.

  — *Reese Davis*

- **'Tis the marrow makes the soup.** There is no soul to the broth without marrow — ham fat or suet may do for some, but for me there's naught like a bone for richness.

  — *Paidric Gallagher*

- **To fatten a snapping turtle, dump him in a swill barrel.** He will proceed to eat gluttonously and soon will be unable to retract his neck and legs due to added weight.   — *Old Nels*

- **Surely, the drink is the curse of the Irish.** It certainly has cost me dear, but then again, the best times I ever had were under the influence!

  — *Paidric Gallagher*

A toast to your health.

The Recipe 500 Readers Tried to Interpret

Our advice: Read the 3 winners,
then do it your own way . . .

THE 1976 EDITION of the Almanac presented a rather famous recipe for Democratic Cake, taken from a 1760s cookbook put out by Dr. Nathaniel Ames of Dedham, Massachusetts. We offered prizes of $15, $10, and $5 for the three best "interpretations" of the original into a recipe that modern cooks would be able to follow.

Dr. Nathaniel Ames's famous Democratic Cake recipe could have been part of the curriculum for these young ladies, who gathered for classes in the art of housekeeping during the mid 1880s. All were from socially prominent families in Detroit.

The original recipe, the Almanac said at the time, offered a "challenge" to present-day cooks. It went like this: "3 qts. flour; 1 lb. butter; 1½ sugar; 1¼ raisins; 4 eggs; ½ glass wine; 1 glass brandy; ½ oz. cinnamon; some corianders; ¼ allspice. Yeast 1 glass or half a jill set rising overnight — and next morning work the sugar and butter together half an hour at least, it will make your cake lighter and whiter. After it has puf'd up light, work in the rest except the raisins, which add at setting into oven."

Dr. Ames's old-time "Democratic" (in contrast to "Royal") Cake inspired more than 500 *Old Farmer's Almanac* readers to submit recipes; the winning

Plain honey left on your lips overnight will have the same effect as petroleum jelly —leaving them moist and shiny. Only honey definitely makes for tastier dreams.

– 1977 –
MARGARET ROSS

The original recipe, the Almanac said, offered a "challenge" to present-day cooks.

recipes appeared in the 1977 edition. The original ingredients would have been whole grain flour, bolted or sifted; sourdough yeast; partially refined sugar or maple sugar; and raisins on the stem, which would have had to be seeded. The hot brick oven of the 1760s would have gradually cooled down as the cake baked; for this reason, we suggest lowering the oven temperature after the first 15 minutes.

Here are three different methods for making the cake — all tasty and all receiving prizes. Each makes 2 small loaves of bread or 1 cake baked in a 10-inch iron skillet.

RECIPE #1

1 package dry yeast	¾ cup raisins
3 cups flour	2 tablespoons brandy
Water or milk	1 tablespoon sweet wine
¼ pound butter	1 teaspoon cinnamon
¾ cup sugar	½ teaspoon allspice
1 large egg	Ground coriander seed

Mix the yeast with 1 cup flour and enough water or milk to make a light sponge. Let the mixture rise overnight. The next morning, cream the butter and sugar, add them to the sponge, and let the dough rise half an hour. Add the rest of the ingredients. Form the dough into loaves. Allow to rise, then bake them for 15 minutes at 375°F; reduce heat to 350° and bake 30 minutes more. — *Alice M. Johnson, Farmington, Utah*

RECIPE #2

¾ cup milk	1 tablespoon wine
¼ cup water	¼ pound butter
1 package dry yeast	1 large egg
¾ cup sugar	1 teaspoon cinnamon
3 cups all-purpose flour	½ teaspoon allspice
¾ cup raisins	Ground coriander seed
2 tablespoons brandy	

To prepare the sponge, scald the milk, then let it cool until it is lukewarm. While it is cooling, heat the water to 110°F, then sprinkle the yeast into the water. Stir in 1 teaspoon sugar. Let the mixture stand until the yeast is working well (5 to 10 minutes), then add it to the milk. Stir in 1 cup flour and beat the mixture until it is smooth. Cover the bowl with a cloth and set it in a warm place until it has doubled in volume.

To prepare the raisins, presoak them, then simmer them with the brandy and wine. Set the mixture aside to cool.

To prepare the cake, cream the butter and the remaining sugar together. Beat the egg, then add it to the butter mixture and mix well. Sift the remaining 2 cups flour with the cinnamon and allspice, then add the sifted ingredients to the butter mixture. Mix in the sponge, raisins, and corianders. Place in greased pans and let rise until doubled in bulk. Bake at 375°F for about 15 minutes, then at 350° for 30 minutes more.

— *H. C. Zettlemoyer,*
Lake Zurich, Illinois

RECIPE #3

1 package dry yeast
1 cup warm water
3 cups flour
¼ pound butter
¾ cup sugar
1 large egg, beaten
1 teaspoon cinnamon
½ teaspoon allspice
Ground coriander seed
1 tablespoon wine
2 tablespoons brandy
¾ cup raisins

Sprinkle the yeast on the warm water. Add 1 cup flour; mix it well into the soft dough. Cover with a cloth and leave in a warm place to rise overnight. Cream the butter and sugar together. Add the egg, spices, wine, and brandy to the butter and sugar. Mix well. Combine the butter mixture with the yeast dough, adding 2 cups flour a little at a time. Knead with the raisins and put in greased baking pans. Cover and let rise until doubled in bulk. Bake at 375°F for 15 minutes, then at 350° for 30 minutes more, or until done.

— *Catherine Gaal,*
New Brunswick, New Jersey ✸

Wise Words for the Good Cook

Y OU MAY MAKE houses enchantingly beautiful, hang them with pictures, have them clean and airy and convenient; but if the stomach is fed with sour bread and burnt meats, it will raise such rebellions that the eyes will see no beauty anywhere." **(1869)**

"A COOK must be quick and strong of sight, her hearing most acute, that she may be sensible when the contents of her vessels bubble . . . and that she may be alarmed before the pot boils over; her auditory nerve ought to discriminate (when several saucepans are in operation at the same time) the simmering of one, the ebullition of another, and the full-toned warbling of a third. . . . It is from the exquisite sensibility of her palate that we admire and judge of the cook." **(1827)**

"For PIES, cakes, and white bread, the heat of the oven should be such that you can hold your hand and arm in while you count forty; for brown bread, meats, beans, Indian puddings, and pumpkin pies, it should be hotter, so that you can hold it in while you count twenty." **(1852)**

On Behalf of Bulldog Gravy

Some call it white gravy or milk gravy. And, sure, it's simple to make. But if you want to do it right, you have to know a few tricks.

By Deborah Navas

My friend John, who was raised in rural North Carolina, had a childhood friend locally famous for his marksmanship and great strength. John's friend could shoot a bumblebee on the wing with a .22 rifle, he lifted the back end of a mired Ford pickup once, and like many Appalachian farm children in lean times, John's friend grew up on bulldog gravy. It's the common opinion among Appalachian Mountain communities that if it weren't for bulldog gravy, a lot of little babies would have died of malnutrition.

Southerners raised outside certain parts of Appalachia may not recognize it by that name, although a good many of them eat bulldog gravy with each meal every day of their lives. Bulldog gravy is also called "white gravy" and "milk gravy." In some high-toned southern cookbooks, it's called "country gravy." But in most places, it's simply "gravy," as in "biscuits and gravy," as common and taken for granted on rural southern dinner tables as salt and pepper.

The ingredients are modest and easily come by on a farm: meat drippings thickened with flour, then milk beaten in to achieve gravy consistency, plus salt and plenty of pepper for seasoning. Bacon and sausage drippings (or lard if no drippings are handy) are most common for breakfast biscuits and gravy, but bulldog gravy does service for dinner and supper as well. You use steak drippings for gravy served with chicken-fried steak — that's a slice of round steak breaded and fried like chicken — and many southerners also serve bulldog gravy with fried chicken itself. A woman I know in northern Arkansas, locally famous for her fried chicken and gravy, confided that she adds a pinch of sugar for seasoning.

Of course, you can add anything you want to bulldog gravy, and crumbled sausage meat is popular. In a recent dinner-table conversation on the subject of bulldog gravy, a friend volunteered that she knew a woman who added chocolate syrup to her gravy, served over biscuits, because she had nothing else in the house that day to start her boy off to school. Since that conversation, I've talked to two other southerners who take their bulldog gravy with chocolate flavoring or make it with chocolate milk.

Although no one I spoke to can say for sure, it's a matter of agreement, and makes some sense, that bulldog gravy originated in areas of rural poverty. It is documented, however, that during the 1930s, striking miners in coal mining areas around Kentucky subsisted on beans and bulldog gravy alone. "[It's] the single contribution to world cuisine of the highland South," Ben Kimpel, a late University of Arkansas scholar, put it.

The "highland South" Kimpel referred to is the Cumberland Mountains, the Blue Ridge Mountains, the southern Appalachian Mountains,

> People eat finicky nowadays. When I was young, we relished blood sausage, brains and eggs, sheep-head soup, fish-head chowder, kidney stew, and mountain oysters —all good, solid, nourishing foods. Yet today's youngsters couldn't be paid to eat them.
>
> – 1930 –
> MRS. A. KELLER,
> AGE 98

and the Ozarks. But bulldog gravy has long since made its way down to the more affluent flatlands, the southern coast, and at least as far west as Texas and Oklahoma. There are few breakfast counters anywhere in the South that don't feature biscuits and gravy on the menu, and that includes McDonald's, whose southern franchises serve more biscuits with gravy than Egg McMuffins.

Because people have become wary of saturated fats, most public eating places now make their bulldog gravy with a vegetable oil or shortening base. Jerry's Restaurant in Fayetteville, Arkansas, has been serving biscuits and gravy since 1978, and according to Doris, Jerry's wife, people come to Fayetteville from as far away as Little Rock and Fort Smith asking for Jerry's biscuits and gravy. The restaurant uses a margarine-and-flour roux as the gravy's base, Doris said. (For professional reasons, she didn't go into the specifics of preparation.)

Although the ingredients are simple, making a very good bulldog gravy requires experience. The *White Trash Cooking* cookbook (Ten Speed Press, 1986) advises: "Always keep reminding yourself that it takes years of practice to make a good gravy. Nobody's perfect right at the very first." Sue McKay, who makes gravy for the University of Arkansas Food Services, agreed. Sue's gravy is reported to be absolutely first-rate. She starts in at five o'clock every morning to make gravy at Brough Commons, a dining hall that serves students, faculty, university employees, and anyone willing to pay a nominal fee for a serving of one fresh-baked baking powder biscuit topped with as much gravy as he or she wants.

The real trick to good gravy, according to Sue, is browning the roux. In an electric skillet, Sue melts about one-third the amount of margarine she'll use, gets it real hot, and with a whip beats in flour ("I measure by guess and by God," she said). "To get that certain flavor, the roux has to brown real good, almost to the burning point." Sue can tell when it's right by the color, "a little darker than caramel." Then she adds the skillet roux to a somewhat larger amount of a margarine-and-flour mixture that she's already prepared in a five-gallon steamer (the margarine and flour in this pot have been beaten together over low heat but not browned). Sue stirs it all together, then adds salt and pepper and beats in the whole milk. When the gravy's ready, she divides it into two pots and adds cooked crumbled sausage to one pot.

"The sausage gravy's most popular," Sue said, "but they love the plain, too. The kids love it, it's cheap and filling, and I've had instructors tell me it's the best in town." (Sue makes her gravy in volume, but if you want to try her method for a batch of gravy that will serve 4, use 2 tablespoons mar-

A quarter-pound hamburger, bun, fries, and a Coke will cost 1,427 gallons of water —and that doesn't count the water used to manufacture and distribute the packaging materials involved.

– 1979 –

garine, 2 tablespoons flour, ½ teaspoon salt, ¼ teaspoon pepper, and 1½ cups milk.)

Sue came by her expertise naturally — she's an Arkansas native, born in Chula, "a little town that's nowhere on the map." When I asked her if she had grown up eating biscuits and gravy, she said, "Well sure, didn't everybody?"

If the demand at the University of Arkansas Food Services is any indication, everybody — at least those south of the Mason-Dixon Line — still does. ✸

There'll Be Times When the Best Choice for You Is Beans

For example . . .

WHEN HENRY DAVID THOREAU made his memorable walking tour down lower Cape Cod, Massachusetts, in 1849, he marveled at the great quantities of codfish spread out to dry at Provincetown. He visited one fish house and wrote: "The cod in this fish-house, just out of the pickle, lay packed several feet deep, and three or four men stood on them in cowhide boots, pitching them on to the barrows with an instrument which had a single iron point. One young man, who chewed tobacco, spat on the fish repeatedly. Well, sir, thought I, when that older man sees you he will speak to you. But presently I saw the older man do the same thing. . . .

" 'How long does it take to cure these fish?' I asked.

" 'Two good drying days, sir,' was the answer.

"I walked across the street again into the hotel to breakfast and mine host inquired if I would take 'hashed fish or beans.' I took beans, though they never were a favorite dish of mine."

Washing the catch in Provincetown, forty years after Thoreau's visit.

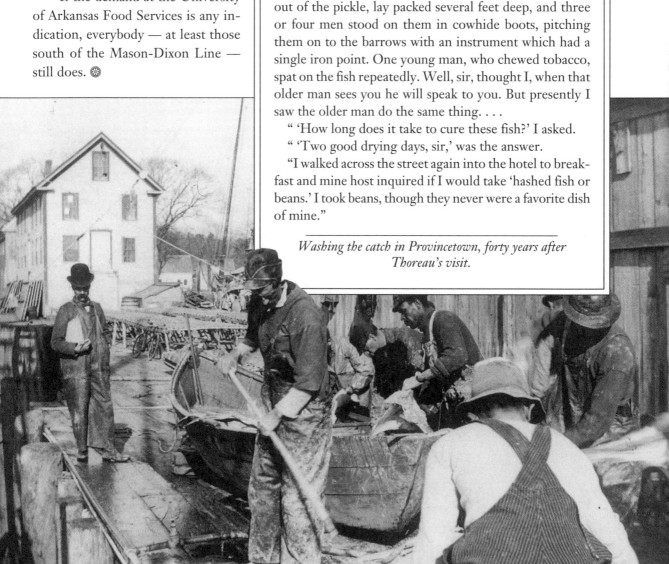

Everything You Always Wanted to Know About Cheesecake

(PLUS THE BEST CHEESECAKE RECIPE IN THE WORLD)

The truth is that a single serving of cheesecake contains the equivalent of the daily caloric intake of many Third World villages. But oh, it is, as the poet said, "a foretaste of heaven."

BY BOB TREBILCOCK

The golden age of modern cheesecake was the 1940s and 1950s, when scrumptious examples like this were the dessert of choice at New York's fashionable Broadway haunt, Lindy's.

GREW UP in the Midwest in the 1960s, in an era before all Americans were transformed into gourmets. No one-inch-diameter medallions of salmon floated in a perfect pond of saffron cream at our house. We ate real food for real people. Now and then my mother prepared some recipe clipped from the rotogravure section of the Sunday newspaper — usually cream-of-mushroom-soup casseroles and adventuresome concoctions with Jell-O.

These attempts to bring a little panache to the table were usually followed the next night with a moist pot roast and tasty apple pie over which otherwise law-abiding citizens might commit the most heinous crime to ensure seconds. You could say that we were food traditionalists who took solace in the conformity of our meals the way businessmen find comfort in the blue suit.

It comes as no surprise, then, that the first cheesecake to find its way to the table met with some skepticism. It was Thanksgiving Day 1969. No one really dug in until halftime of the second football game — after the apple, pumpkin, and mincemeat pies were gone. No doubt there was a little regional snobbery involved here. Cheesecake was prefaced with the words "New York style," and to a midwesterner, the last good thing to come out of New York City was the Dodgers, and they had had the good sense to move west.

But we were wrong about cheesecake. The experience was an epiphany for our taste buds. From then on, holiday dessert for me meant rich, creamy cheesecake. Some thought I was a little fanatical when I insisted my wife-to-be apprentice with my mother, but in cheese-

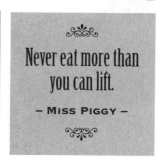

Never eat more than you can lift.

– MISS PIGGY –

cake and marriage, you can't be too careful. *The Dictionary of Calories and Carbohydrates* (Grosset & Dunlap, 1973) claims that a 4-ounce serving of commercial cheesecake contains only 306 calories. Of course, they are dealing with a miserly portion of the kind of airy impostor that resembles the real thing in name only. The truth is, a single serving — what I consider a single serving, at least — contains the equivalent of the daily caloric intake of most Third World villages. I'm certain cheesecake was on the mind of the church when gluttony was designated as one of the seven deadly sins.

The history of cheesecake is almost as rich as its flavor. The ancient Greeks most likely invented the delicacy more than two thousand years ago: cottage cheese put through a sieve was blended with honey and flour and baked until done. The Greeks accurately described their culinary contribution as "dainty food for mortal man." According to food writer M. F. K. Fisher, prospective grooms in Argos were presented with cheesecakes prior to the wedding, presumably as the eating experience most closely resembling the joys of an evening of frolic.

The Romans knew a good thing when they saw it. Cato, the Roman soldier and statesman, included a cheesecake recipe with his booty from the conquest of Greece. The recipe survives; in fact, at least one scholar of culinary history (namely me) has wondered whether the decline of the Roman Empire might be traced to a preoccupation with cheesecake.

The author's favorite cheesecake is, naturally, his mother's. (Turn to page 52 for the recipe.) It's especially good served one day old and topped with strawberries.

The Dark Ages, of course, were not nearly as dark as is often thought. Cheesecake not only survived, but in pre-Renaissance England it thrived. In 1381, a recipe for cheesecake was published in the *Book of the Table*, leading one English poet to describe the dessert as "a foretaste of heaven with glimpses of higher life and ethereal worlds."

Of course, cheesecake evolution wasn't limited to England. The Italians perfected a ricotta pie with candied fruit, and the Russians developed *pashka*, a traditional cottage cheese or cream cheese dessert served at Easter. Although it's rarely reported, cheesecake played an important role in the French Revolution when Marie Antoinette was mistakenly beheaded after the erroneous report that she said the peasants should eat cake. What she actually said was, "Let them eat cheesecake," a sign not of royal indifference to the masses, but of genuine benevolence.

The first published recipe for the modern dessert we know as cheesecake was probably the one included in Mrs. Glasse's *Art of Cookery Made Plain and Simple*, published in the late 1700s. Early cheesecakes were a rough cousin to the smooth concoction we eat today. The breakthrough came in 1872, when New York dairymen invented cream cheese while attempting to duplicate the flavor of unripened French Neufchâtel. The proprietors of New York's Jewish delicatessens used the new cheese to bake a rich cake with a zwieback or graham-cracker crust.

For a time it looked as if the new dessert might be available only to the rich and famous. Then, on August 27, 1926, the *New York Times* reported that a cartel known as the Brownsville and East New York Cream Cheese Dealers' Association had been broken up. Israel M. Lerner, the state deputy attorney general, predicted a 30 percent reduction in the price of the most crucial ingredient. Cheesecake lovers across the Big Apple cheered.

By the mid-1940s, the dessert was popular enough to support a growing number of businesses devoted only to cheesecake. The dessert of choice at Lindy's, the fashionable Broadway haunt of the 1940s and 1950s, was cheesecake. The Lindy's recipe was printed in *Good Housekeeping* and other far-reaching publications, and the moniker "New York style" became as permanently attached to cheesecake as Kansas City to a strip steak.

That was the golden age of cheesecake. In today's era of designer foods and pizzas with marinated cactus and duck liv-

Happiness Comes from the Simple Things

For example . . .

By Alan Devoe

IT IS CHARACTERISTIC of life in quiet country places that everyday incidents are seldom very large. And it is characteristic, too, of those who elect to live in such places that they find the most moving moments of their lives, and the wellspring of their profoundest happiness, in small and unspectacular happenings.

I recollect that someone once observed of W. H. Davies, the English poet, that "his whole gospel of content is a cup of tea in a country cottage." This, perhaps, is rather too strictly limited to be a quite serviceable gospel. I have no quarrel with the cup of tea, but I would expand the thing a little to include — after the tea or before it — walks.

The walks need not, with the farm as their start and end, be very long. They may be the briefest and most casual affairs — stray putterings in nearby woods when the vireos are nesting, strolls across meadowland when killdeer are running and crying there, walks through pine groves when the snow lies deep. Grant these, and I rather think that the gospel has no peer.

ers, cheesecake has gone exotic. Lately I've found cheesecake recipes with whole-wheat crusts (whom are they trying to kid?); fillings of blue cheese, Gouda, cottage cheese, ricotta, avocado, buttermilk, cider, tofu, and pumpkin; cheesecakes topped with daiquiris, grapefruit, passion fruit, currants, and cranberries. There is something called Cheesecake Alaska with Pistachio Filling, as well as recipes for low-calorie cheesecake and cheesecake in a flowerpot. Under the headline " . . . Something Completely Different," the *New York Times* once published a recipe for smoked salmon and onion cheesecake. And for the do-it-yourselfer, how about "Your Own Cheese, Your Own Cake." That implies your own cow raised on your own farm. No, thanks — I don't want to get into farming just for dessert.

It's not that I wouldn't try any of these cheesecakes; I'm ecumenical enough to paraphrase Will Rogers's comment on people and say I've never met a cheesecake I didn't like. But in a perfect world, I'd prefer mine served like red wines and German beers: in quantity, plain, and warmed almost to room temperature. With that in mind, I offer my mother's cheesecake recipe. It's simple, rich, and delicious. I think it tastes best when served a day old. My mother prepares it a day earlier than needed, usually so late at night that my father goes to bed rather than wait for it to cool.

VIRGINIA TREBILCOCK'S CHEESECAKE

CRUST

2 cups crushed graham crackers

½ cup butter, melted
¼ cup crushed walnuts

FILLING

3 packages (8 ounces each) cream cheese, at room temperature

1½ cups sugar
5 eggs
3 tablespoons lemon juice

TOPPING

1 pint sour cream
½ cup sugar

1 teaspoon vanilla

Preheat the oven to 350°F. Combine the crust ingredients and press them evenly against the bottom and sides of a 10-inch springform pan.

To make the filling, combine the cream cheese and sugar. Add the eggs one at a time, beating thoroughly after each one. Beat in the lemon juice. Pour the filling over the crust and bake for 45 minutes without opening the oven door.

Remove the cheesecake and reduce the oven temperature to 300°F. Combine the topping ingredients and spread the topping over the cheesecake. Return the cake to the oven and bake for 15 minutes. Cool on a rack for several hours, then refrigerate overnight. Serve plain or topped with fruit. ⊛

The One Good Way to Keep Your Boiled Lobster from Dying in Agony

A recent study says that lobsters don't have enough brain for pain. But can we be sure?

MANY PEOPLE (including us) identify a lobster's frantic tail flipping as a sign of pain when it's being introduced to a steaming or boiling pot. But now a University of Maine researcher, Michael Loughlin, says that the lobster's temperature sensors that trigger the wiggling reflex are not a brain and that because lobsters don't have a cerebral cortex, their ability to experience pain is nonexistent. Nonetheless, on the advice of Professor Robert Bayer of the university's Animal, Veterinary, and Aquatic Sciences Department, he decided to conduct an experiment to see if tail flipping during the cooking process could be reduced. Just in case.

Accordingly, Loughlin volunteered his services as a chef to anyone on campus who wanted a lobster dinner. He ended up with two hundred takers.

On the appointed day, he first steamed a bunch of lobsters on racks inside a large pot. He found that the lobsters on the top racks stayed alive — and continued wiggling — much longer than the ones on the bottom. Some were alive twenty minutes after the ones on the bottom were cooked. Yikes.

Next he hypnotized some lobsters (by turning them upside down and stroking their little tails) before dropping them into boiling water. The thrashing about lasted up to ninety seconds. Not good.

His third experiment consisted of putting lobsters into warm water and then gradually turning up the heat. Bad. All the lobsters feverishly tail-flipped for a very long time.

Finally, he put a half dozen lobsters on ice for fifteen minutes and then suddenly dropped them all into water brought to a rolling boil. Voilà! None of them wiggled or thrashed about for more than thirty seconds, and some didn't move at all.

CHAPTER 3

Around the Dining Room Table

MOST DINING ROOM advice in the old Almanacs had to do with manners, and each rule invariably contained the word "don't." Don't smell your meat or dip it into a sauce; don't throw anything under the table; don't spit, cough, or blow your nose during a meal; don't pick your teeth—unless, with your other hand, you hold a napkin in front of your mouth. And so on.

Certainly these are well-known rules today, even if they're not always followed to the letter. Therefore, much of this chapter deals with an entirely different aspect of dining room behavior: the always-tricky art of conversation. Like when you've been seated between two strangers at a formal dinner party knowing that each one's good impression of you could benefit, say, your career. And yet you feel you have nothing to say. Perhaps a careful reading of the following pages will prove to be of some assistance. ❁

Those awkward moments at a dinner party often require special skills.

How to Appear to Know More Than You Really Do

Like the great matador, the torero of the dining room table is marked by his (or her) ability to dodge, to weave, to dance on the edge of disaster. Here, from an expert, are the basics.

By Tim Clark

*I*T IS A FAMILIAR SCENE. We have just come home from a dinner party, and my wife is disconsolate. "I'm too stupid to live," she moans.

"You're not *that* stupid," I say. "What do you mean?" (I know exactly what she means, but for the purposes of exposition, I shall feign ignorance.)

"At dinner everyone was talking about books and movies and politics, and you all know so much about them," she says. "I just sit there like a lump. I haven't read the books or seen the movies, and politics just makes me want to scream."

Yes, she has a problem all right. But it's not the problem she thinks it is. Her shortcoming has nothing to do with her intellect, which is keen. It has everything to do with her one tragic character flaw: she is honest.

Now, in spite of this, I love her madly. But candor is a crippling deficiency in polite social intercourse. Don't misunderstand me — I'm not advocating lying. Lying is immoral. Lying is unethical. Lying can get you caught. And finally, lying is too easy. We are talking about a high art here, an art akin to bullfighting. Like the great matador, the *torero* of the dining room table is marked by his (or her) ability to dodge, to weave, to dance on the edge of disaster.

I once met a man whose impudence and skill at evading the on-rushing horns of his interrogators made me want to shout, "Olé!"

If, for example, someone asked him, "Have you read *Don Quixote?*" he would say, "Not recently." Of course, he'd never read it at all, but why disrupt a perfectly congenial conversation?

On another occasion, when asked if he had read Dante's *Inferno*, he replied, "Not in English." I was awestruck. In three absolutely truthful words, he managed to convey three distinct and misleading messages: (1) that he had read the book; (2) that he was fluent in Italian; and (3) that he was the sort of literary purist who would never settle for a mere translation. Glorious. I believe that, in certain countries, my friend would have been awarded the ears and tail of the person who asked the question.

But you don't have to be Manolete to sling the bull. All you have to do is memorize a few Safe Subjects, All-Purpose Adjectives, Multifaceted Facts, and Irrefutable Opinions.

SAFE SUBJECTS

A safe subject is one that is interesting and provocative enough to allow you to make broad statements of dubious value (nobody wants to listen to you expound on the fine points of nineteenth-century German foreign

When your dinner partner asks if you've ever read Dante's Inferno *(that's Dante, above), a suitable reply might be, "Not in English."*

The quantum physics theories of Niels Bohr (left) are Safe Subjects because it's unlikely anyone will know what you're talking about. The topic even confused Einstein (right).

policy or discuss the nuances of Kwakiutl creation myths), but at the same time is obscure or complicated enough that nobody but an expert will be able to call your bluff. (It's always a good idea to circulate among the guests before dinner and engage in a little light conversation about their interests so that you know which subjects to avoid. I once held forth for twenty minutes on my interpretation of the Chinese Cultural Revolution — unencumbered by facts — all the while unaware that the man sitting next to me was the nation's leading authority on Chinese history. It was not an experience I'd care to repeat.)

Here are a few Safe Subjects you might wish to consider:

1. Quantum physics: For ambiguity, it's hard to beat. It gave Einstein fits, and the best-known part of it is something called The Uncertainty Principle. The father of quantum physics, Niels Bohr, was famous for making cryptic remarks about the nature of reality, then giggling uncontrollably at the look on his students' faces (see "What to Do When Confronted").

2. The Dead Sea Scrolls: Discovered in 1947, these ancient texts have been studied ever since by a small group of biblical scholars who won't let anyone else take a look, probably because they still haven't figured out what they mean.

3. James Knox Polk: One of a series of one-term presidents preceding the Civil War, he was elected in 1844 and declined to run for a second term. Not very interesting in himself, he's a convenient guy to bring up if you get tired of somebody at the table who is yammering on about the current occupant of the White House. Then *you* say, "What about James Knox Polk?"

The person talking is stopped cold. "What about him?" he says belligerently.

"Well, everything you just said could also apply to James Knox Polk," you reply. "And look what happened to him. He declined to run for a second term."

Everyone nods. Who could argue with that?

ALL-PURPOSE ADJECTIVES

These are descriptive terms that apply to almost anything. When asked to comment on a book, play, film, or musical composition of which you are completely ignorant, you should say:

"I prefer his (her) earlier works. They're more *pristine*." (Relatively few people know what "pristine" means. One of its meanings is "earlier.")

Or, alternatively:

"I prefer her (his) later works. They're more *mature*."

MULTIFACETED FACTS

You can sound learned without being verbose. The strategic insertion of a single unusual piece of information can leave your fellow diners with a lasting impression of erudition. For example, the author

CONVERSATION ENHANCERS

How Old Is an Old Chestnut?

A EUROPEAN CHESTNUT standing on the slopes of Mount Etna in Sicily had a girth of 204 feet and was estimated to be more than 2,000 years old. It was later destroyed during an eruption, thus proving that lava conquers all.

In this country, there is hardly a live American chestnut to be found, due to the chestnut blight (*Endothia parasitica*), which began along the Atlantic seaboard around the turn of the century. So the next time someone derides one of your comments as "an old chestnut," remind him or her that in this part of the world, an old chestnut is a rare and valuable item.

Chestnutting, *by Winslow Homer.*

Casual mention of the connection between Manfred von Richthofen, D.H. Lawrence, and Snoopy can favorably impress fellow diners.

D. H. Lawrence's wife, Frieda, was the sister of Baron von Richthofen, the famous German flying ace. This is a valuable piece of trivia because it can be dropped casually into a discussion of any of the following subjects:

1. D. H. Lawrence
2. The "Red Baron"
3. Twentieth-century English literature
4. World War I
5. In-laws
6. Sex (any reference to D. H. Lawrence is appropriate in this area)
7. Snoopy

IRREFUTABLE OPINIONS

At some point in any dinner conversation, someone is bound to turn to you and say, "What do you think?"

You don't want to say what you really think, because you haven't been paying attention. You have actually been thinking about the funny noise you heard in your car on the way over, or wondering why your hostess bought that hideous painting on the wall, or trying to remember the name of the actress who played Mary Ann on "Gilligan's Island." But you can't admit that. This is where you need to express an opinion that is relevant to any subject, and impervious to contradiction. Here are three good ones:

"It all depends."

"You can't generalize."

"Things are different in the South."

WHAT TO DO WHEN CONFRONTED

Even under the best of circumstances, some rude person may try to embarrass you by pointing out that you are a fraud. Don't panic. You have three options:

1. Tell the following anecdote: Niels Bohr (that master of obscurity) once said there are two kinds of truth, trivial and profound. The opposite of a trivial truth is a falsehood. The opposite of a profound truth is *another profound truth*. Then you can excuse yourself from the table while your questioner is trying to figure out what you just said.

2. Point out the nearest window and shout, "Look at that!" hoping to distract the company's attention. The hazard in this scheme is that you may succeed too well. A friend tried it, and when everyone turned to the window, they saw two dogs sharing a moment of intimacy in the back yard.

3. Take a bite of meat and chew it thoughtfully, as if formulating your reply. Then, once it is well chewed and tucked in a corner of your mouth, simulate choking to death. Hold your breath, pointing frantically at your throat. If possible, turn blue. Rush out of the dining room and hurl yourself stomach-first against the back of a sofa or divan. You may want to do this two or three times, so that everyone will understand that you are performing the Heimlich maneuver *on yourself*. When you judge the moment to be right, spit the concealed bit of meat into your napkin with a realistic retching sound, straighten up, turn to the horrified onlookers, and calmly say, "I'm all right." If performed persuasively, this will cause everyone present to forget the unfortunate incident that precipitated your problem and congratulate you on your presence of mind. Olé! ☣

Why Is It So Hard to Get Ketchup Out of a Bottle?

To answer this, we must first agree on what we mean by a liquid. Let's say that a liquid is any sort of stuff that flows when you pour it. But if you take a bottle of ketchup from the shelf, unscrew the top, and turn the bottle on its head — it does not flow. Must we infer from this that it is not a liquid?

Now take up the bottle, replace the top, and vigorously shake the bottle — vigorously in the style of a barman shaking a cocktail. When you remove the top again, you can readily pour the ketchup out of the bottle.

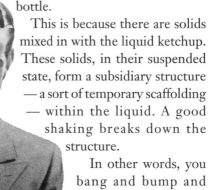

This is because there are solids mixed in with the liquid ketchup. These solids, in their suspended state, form a subsidiary structure — a sort of temporary scaffolding — within the liquid. A good shaking breaks down the structure.

In other words, you bang and bump and shake the bottle. First nothing'll come — then a lottle.

The Night I Had Dinner with George Washington

This is an eyewitness account from the journal of William Maclay,
U.S. senator from Pennsylvania, 1789–1791.

> When a man
> says, "I lie," does
> he lie or does he
> speak the truth?
> If he lies, he speaks
> the truth; if he speaks
> the truth, he lies.
>
> – 1870 –

AUGUST 27, 1789: Senate adjourned early. At a little after four, I called on Mr. Bassett of the Delaware State. He and I went to the President's dinner. The company were: President and Mrs. Washington, Vice President and Mrs. Adams, the Governor and his wife, Mr. Jay and wife, Mr. Langdon and wife, Dr. Dalton and a lady (perhaps his wife), and a Mr. Smith, Mr. Bassett, myself, Lear, Lewis, the President's two secretaries. The President and Mrs. Washington

Left to right: George Washington; his step-grandson, George Washington Parke Custis; his step-granddaughter, Eleanor; and his wife, Martha. Martha, of course, was married once before wedding George — who, although the Father of Our Country, was never actually a father.

sat opposite each other in the middle of the table; the two secretaries, one at each end. It was a great dinner, and the best of the kind I ever was at. The room, however, was disagreeably warm.

First was the soup; then fish roasted and boiled; meats, gammon, fowls, etc. This was the dinner. The middle of the table was garnished in the usual tasty way with small images, flowers (artificial), etc. The dessert was first apple pies, pudding, etc.; then iced creams, jellies, etc.; then watermelons, muskmelons, apples, peaches, nuts.

It was the most solemn dinner I ever sat at. Not a health drank; scarce a word said until the cloth was taken away. Then the President, filling a glass of wine, with great formality drank the health of every individual by name 'round the table. Everybody imitated him, charged glasses, and such a buzz of "health, sir," and "thank you, madam," never had I heard before. Indeed, I had liked to have been thrown out in the hurry; but I got a little wine in my glass and passed the ceremony. The ladies sat a good while, and the bottles passed about; but there was a dead silence almost. Mrs. Washington at last withdrew with the ladies.

I expected the men would now begin, but the same stillness remained. The President told of a New England clergyman who had lost a hat and wig in passing a river called the Brunks. He smiled, and everybody else laughed. . . . There was a Mr. Smith, who mentioned how *Homer* described *Aeneas* leaving his wife and carrying his father out of flaming Troy. He had heard somebody (I suppose) witty on the occasion; but if he had ever read it he would have said *Virgil*. The President kept a fork in his hand, when the cloth was taken away, I thought for the purpose of picking nuts. He ate no nuts, however, but played with the fork, striking the edge of the table with it. We did not sit long after the ladies retired. The President rose, went upstairs to drink coffee; the company followed. I took my hat and come home. ✽

George Washington's Christmas Eggnog

In his own words . . .

ONE QUART CREAM, 1 quart milk, 1 dozen tablespoons sugar, 1 pint brandy, ½ pint rye whiskey, ½ pint Jamaica rum, ¼ pint sherry — mix liquor first, then separate yolks and whites of eggs, add sugar to beaten yolks, mix well. Add liquor to mixture drop by drop at first, slowly beating. Add milk and cream, slowly beating. Beat whites of eggs until stiff and fold slowly into mixture. Let set in cool place for several days. Taste frequently."

Courtesy of Dick O'Donnell, Honolulu, Hawaii.

How Happy Is a Clam?

By Tim Clark

W<small>E WILL PROBABLY</small> never know exactly what makes a clam happy, but people usually list a long life and true love among their hopes. Thus, by human standards, a clam has good reason to be happy, because according to Ida Thompson of Princeton University, the clam is the foxy grandpa of the invertebrate kingdom. Thompson has determined that the bands one finds on a clamshell correspond to the rings found in a tree trunk and can be used to determine the clam's age. By this method, she has discovered that clams live as long as 150 years (assuming they are not made into chowder), show no signs of aging (other than adding bands), and remain sexually active throughout their lives. In fact, Thompson is uncertain whether clams ever die of old age.

Raking for happy clams at low tide.

William Penn,
who introduced the
Quaker faith into
America, had his own
private brewery.

– 1979 –

Dining by the Calendar

*Everyone knows the foods traditionally associated with major
holidays like Thanksgiving and Christmas, but here is a guide to
the appropriate meals for dozens of lesser-known holidays.*

By E. Brady

THERE ARE DOZENS of holidays, some virtually forgotten today, which in diverse times and places have been celebrated with special foods. Some practices probably arose from the fruits available in the season, rather than from the nature of the holiday itself. In England, geese fed on the stubble remaining from harvest were at their fattest just in time for the feast of St. Martin on November 11 — the last festal opportunity to gorge before the Advent fast. Other customs derive from circumstances associated with the event or saint being celebrated: shellfish for St. James the fisherman or beer for St. Dunstan, patron saint of brewers.

A few of these traditions are best left unexplored. The old custom of baking round loaves to be blessed for St. Agatha's Day (February 5) in parts of Europe seems obscure but pleasant enough — unless you know that the loaves represent the saint's breasts, sliced off when she was martyred.

The following list includes some of the foods associated with feasts and holidays past and present. (Timing of some holidays varies from one year to the next; check the latest edition of *The Old Farmer's Almanac* for this year's exact dates.)

JANUARY

Feast of the Circumcision: Black-eyed peas and pork (United States); oat-husk gruel or oatmeal porridge (Scotland).

Epiphany: Cake with a lucky bean baked in it; the one who finds the bean is the king or queen of the feast, in memory of the three wise men (France).

St. Agnes: Food (especially nuts) used ritually by girls to divine the fidelity of a sweetheart (Great Britain, southern United States). St. Agnes, virgin and martyr, is thought to be particularly indulgent to romantic young girls. The method for the divination is to take two nuts, naming one for yourself and one for your sweetheart. Place both on the grate in the fireplace. If they burn at the same time, he is true; if they fly apart or his fails to burn, he is not.

Robert Burns Day: Haggis — sheep's stomach stuffed with suet, chopped organ meat (heart, lungs, liver), onions, oatmeal, and seasonings

*OPPOSITE: Englishwomen
celebrate Shrove Tuesday
by making pancakes, using
up the last of their eggs
and butter prior to
the Lenten fast.*

In February, St. Agatha is remembered with small, round loaves of bread — a tradition that seems obscure but pleasant enough, unless you know where it came from.

(Scotland). Haggis is a traditional Scottish delicacy served on all holidays of national importance.

FEBRUARY

Candlemas Day: Pancakes eaten today will prevent hemorrhoids for a full year (French-American).

St. Agatha: Round loaves of bread blessed by a priest (southern Europe).

Shrove Tuesday: Pancakes (England); oatcakes (Scotland); rabbit (Ireland). Rich foods are eaten to usher in the Lenten fast; pancakes use up the last of the eggs and butter.

Lent: Simnel, a large fruitcake baked so hard it has sometimes been mistaken by recipients for a hassock or footstool (Great Britain). Originally, these cakes had some religious significance, now long forgotten.

MARCH

St. David: Leeks, to be worn (Wales) or eaten raw (England). Recalls a Welsh victory over the Saxons in A.D. 640; the Welsh wore leeks in their hats to distinguish them from the enemy.

St. Benedict: Nettle soup (ancient monastic practice). The picking of the nettles, which irritate the skin, was a penance in keeping with the spirit of the monastic rule of St. Benedict.

Purim: Strong drink and three-cornered cookies flavored with poppy-seed (Jewish). These cookies, called *hamantaschen*, are said to represent the three-cornered hat of Haman, the enemy of the Jewish people, whose downfall is celebrated in this holiday.

Maundy Thursday: Green foods or foods colored green (southern

Europe). The medieval liturgical observance called for green vestments; in some parts of Europe, it is still called Green Thursday.

Good Friday: Hot cross buns. If made properly on this day, they will never get moldy, even after years (England); even a crumb of any bread baked this day has the power to prevent or cure diarrhea all year (England).

Easter: Lamb as symbol of sacrifice; ham.

APRIL

St. Mark: Nuts used for divination (Great Britain). The nuts are placed in the fireplace as described for the feast of St. Agnes, but each one represents the outcome of any cherished project. The one that burns first is the one that will come to pass.

Beltane, May Day Eve: Strong ale (England); oatcakes with nine knobs to be broken off one by one and offered to each of nine supernatural protectors of domestic animals (Scotland). May Day represents an ancient Indo-European religious feast celebrating through fire the return of summer.

MAY

Ascension Day: Fowl, or pastries molded in the shape of birds, to commemorate the taking of Jesus into the skies (medieval Europe).

Whitsunday (Pentecost): Dove or pigeon in honor of the Holy Spirit (southern Europe); strong ale (England).

St. Dunstan: Beer. Cider pressed today will go bad (England).

Corpus Christi: Orange peel dipped in chocolate, chicken stuffed with sauerkraut (Basque Provinces); origin of the custom unknown.

JUNE

St. Anthony of Padua: Liver, possibly based on pre-Christian custom of eating liver on the summer solstice.

Feast of St. John the Baptist: First fruits of spring harvest eaten; basil or cucumber plants exchanged (Sicily).

JULY

St. Swithin: Eggs, because he miraculously restored intact a basket of eggs that had been broken by a poor woman taking them to market; he also looks after apples (medieval England).

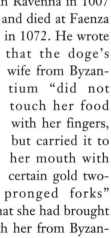

CONVERSATION ENHANCERS

Does Anyone Know the History of the Fork?

By Althea H. Jackson

EARLY IN THE ELEVENTH century, a woman journeyed from Byzantium to the Italian seaport of Venice. In 1070 she married a rich doge, Domenico Selvo. Now it so happens that the first person in written history to mention forks was the Italian St. Peter Damian, who was born in Ravenna in 1007 and died at Faenza in 1072. He wrote that the doge's wife from Byzantium "did not touch her food with her fingers, but carried it to her mouth with certain gold two-pronged forks" that she had brought with her from Byzantium. Everyone was shocked by the lady's extravagance, and few copied her example.

There's more to the history of the fork, but perhaps that's enough for now . . .

Those who would honor St. James eat oysters in July, although here he seems to have a scallop shell.

St. James: Oysters, because James was a fisherman; his symbol has traditionally been a shell (England).

AUGUST

Lammas Day: Oatcakes (Scotland); loaves made from new grain of the season (England); toffee; seaweed pudding. Blueberries in baskets as an offering to a sweetheart are the last vestige of this holiday as a pagan fertility festival (Ireland).

St. Lawrence of Rome: Because the saint was roasted to death on a gridiron, it is courteous to serve only cold meat today (southern Europe).

Feast of the Assumption: Onions, possibly because they have always been considered wholesome and potent against evil (Polish-American).

SEPTEMBER

St. Giles: Tea loaf with raisins (Scotland).

Nativity of Mary: Blackberries, possibly because the color is reminiscent of depictions of the Virgin's blue cloak (Brittany).

Michaelmas Day: New wine (Europe); goose, originally a sacrifice to the saint (Great Britain); cake of oats, barley, and rye (Scotland); carrots (Ireland).

OCTOBER

Rosh Hashanah: Sweet foods; honey; foods colored orange or yellow, to represent a bright, joyous, and sweet new year (Jewish).

St. Faith: Cake of flour, water, salt, and sugar for use in divination; a particle under the pillow imparts prophetic dreams (Great Britain).

Yom Kippur: Fast day; the day before, eat kreplach (filled noodles), considered by generations of mothers to be good and filling (Jewish).

St. Luke: Oatcakes flavored with anise and cinnamon (Scotland).

Sts. Simon and Jude: Dirge cakes, simple fried buns made for distribution to the poor. (Doughnuts are a version of dirge or soul cake.) Also apples or potatoes, for divination (Scotland and England). Divination with apples, as readers of Charles Dickens know, is accomplished by peeling the fruit in one long strip and tossing the peeling over one's shoulder. The letter formed by the peeling is then interpreted.

All Hallows' Eve: Apples and nuts for divination (England); buttered oat-husk gruel (Scotland); *bosty*, a mixture of potatoes, cabbage, and onions (Ireland). The use of apples in Halloween celebrations may be as ancient as the Roman holiday honoring Pomona, goddess of fruit trees, whose festival fell on November 1.

NOVEMBER

All Saints' Day: Chestnuts (Italy); gingerbread and oatcakes (Scotland); milk (central Europe); doughnuts, whose round shape indicates eternity (Tyrol).

All Souls' Day: Skull-shaped candy (Mexico); beans, peas, and lentils, considered food of the poor, as penance for souls in purgatory (southern Europe).

St. Martin: Last religious feast day before beginning of Advent fast. Goose, last of fresh-killed meat before winter; blood pudding. At one time, blood from the butchering was used to mark the corners of the house, protecting it from evil (Great Britain).

St. Andrew: Haggis — stuffed sheep's stomach (Scotland).

DECEMBER

St. Nicholas: Fruit, nuts, candy for children (Germany). Commemorates, in part, the miracle by which the saint restored to life three young boys who had been murdered by a greedy innkeeper.

St. Lucy: Headcheese; cakes flavored with saffron or cardamom, raisins, and almonds (Sweden). The saffron imparts a yellow color to the cakes, representing sunlight, whose return is celebrated at the solstice.

Christmas: Boar's head or goose, plum pudding, nuts, oranges (England); turkey (United States); spiced beef (Ireland).

St. John the Evangelist: Small loaves of bread made with blessed wine (medieval Europe). This is a feast on which wine is ritually blessed in memory of the saint, who drank poisoned wine and miraculously survived.

Hanukkah: Potato pancakes (Jewish).

Holy Innocents' Day: Baby food, pablum, Cream of Wheat, in honor of the children killed by King Herod of Judea (monastic observance).

St. Sylvester: Strong drink (United States); haggis, oatcakes and cheese, oat-husk gruel or porridge (Scotland). ✽

CONVERSATION ENHANCERS

How Fast Is Greased Lightning?

ACCORDING TO *The New Encyclopaedia Britannica*, lightning travels from its point of origin in the sky to the earth's surface at an average speed of 1.5×10^5 meters per second, or about 335,000 miles per hour. Greased lightning is, of course, considerably swifter.

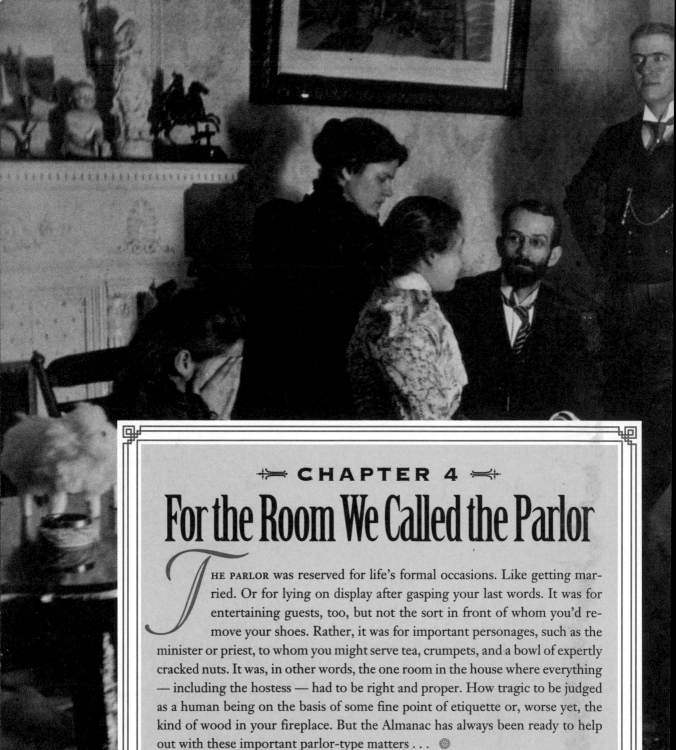

CHAPTER 4

For the Room We Called the Parlor

THE PARLOR was reserved for life's formal occasions. Like getting married. Or for lying on display after gasping your last words. It was for entertaining guests, too, but not the sort in front of whom you'd remove your shoes. Rather, it was for important personages, such as the minister or priest, to whom you might serve tea, crumpets, and a bowl of expertly cracked nuts. It was, in other words, the one room in the house where everything — including the hostess — had to be right and proper. How tragic to be judged as a human being on the basis of some fine point of etiquette or, worse yet, the kind of wood in your fireplace. But the Almanac has always been ready to help out with these important parlor-type matters . . . ✳

Dress and behavior in the parlor were anything but casual.

The True Nature of Crumpets

They are shockingly plain, resemble pancakes, are rather chewy in texture, and, when made correctly, are frightfully good with a spot of tea, served with your best china — in the parlor.

BY JUDY GORMAN

A LONG-TIME FAMILY friend recently remarked that as a child, I was inordinately preoccupied with food. Now that I think about it, I have to agree. For one thing, I was fascinated with the exotic foods described in storybooks. It was at fictional tea parties that I became acquainted with crumpets, which seemed a mysterious, yet elegant, accompaniment to tea. Of course, I had absolutely no idea what crumpets looked like, so I imagined them to be much like sugarplums, raspberry tarts, and other fanciful treats. Consider my surprise when, years later, I discovered their true nature.

Crumpets are shockingly plain. They're about the diameter of an English muffin, and they closely resemble pancakes in thickness and texture. Properly made crumpets are filled with tiny air pockets and have a chewy consistency. Crumpets are produced from a yeast-leavened batter that is allowed to rise until it falls in on itself, a procedure that lends a certain sourdough taste to the final product. A small amount of baking soda is usually stirred into the batter at the last minute to modify the tang; this may be omitted if you prefer a more assertive flavor.

Like pancakes, crumpets are cooked on a griddle. The batter is poured into round metal forms called crumpet rings (available in kitchenware stores; in a pinch, use tuna fish cans with both ends removed) and is heated until the surface is dotted with air holes. Then the rings are lifted off, and each crumpet is flipped to cook the other side.

It is customary to toast crumpets after cooking them. Unlike English muffins, they are never split. They may be cut into halves or quarters before serving. Hot toasted crumpets slathered with butter are delicious eaten out of hand. They also may be topped with jam, jelly, conserve, or fruit butter. A delicious though somewhat unorthodox alternative is to drizzle crumpets with warm maple syrup and eat them with a knife and fork.

Crumpets store well and freeze successfully if wrapped in plastic bags. Homemade crumpets (cooked but not toasted) make a thoughtful gift. Prop a package in a wicker basket alongside a tin of imported tea and drop in on a friend at a propitious moment — such as teatime.

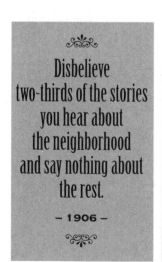

Disbelieve two-thirds of the stories you hear about the neighborhood and say nothing about the rest.

– 1906 –

CRUMPETS

½ cup warm water	2 tablespoons butter
1 package (1 scant tablespoon) dry yeast	½ teaspoon salt
	2 cups all-purpose flour
1 teaspoon sugar	½ teaspoon baking soda
1 cup milk	1 tablespoon tepid water

In a large mixing bowl, combine the ½ cup warm water and the yeast. Add the sugar and stir to dissolve the yeast. Set aside.

In a small saucepan, heat ½ cup of the milk and the butter until the butter melts. Remove the pan from the heat and stir in the salt and the remaining ½ cup milk. Set aside to cool to room temperature.

When cooled, add the milk mixture to the yeast mixture and stir to blend. Mix in the flour with a wooden spoon. The batter will be very lumpy. Cover the bowl with plastic wrap, securing it with a rubber band. Set aside to rise for 1½ hours, or until the bubbling action slows and the mixture begins to collapse in on itself.

Place four crumpet rings on a griddle, allowing the sides to touch. Set over medium heat. Spray all the surfaces lightly with vegetable oil. Dissolve the soda in the 1 tablespoon tepid water and stir into the batter. The batter will be moist and ropy. When the griddle is hot, take up the batter by scant quarter cupfuls and pour it into the rings. Spread the batter to the sides with the back of a spoon.

As the batter begins to set, carefully rotate the rings to ensure even cooking. When the surface of the crumpets is covered with holes and no longer looks wet (about 3 minutes), remove the rings with tongs. Turn the crumpets over and continue cooking for about 1 minute more, or until the surface is lightly browned. Repeat with the remaining batter, spraying the rings and griddle before each batch. Cool the crumpets on a wire rack. Toast before serving. *Makes 10.*

ORANGE CRUMPETS

½ cup warm water	2 tablespoons butter, melted
1 package (1 scant tablespoon) dry yeast	1 tablespoon finely grated orange zest
1 teaspoon sugar	½ teaspoon salt
⅔ cup freshly squeezed orange juice	2 cups all-purpose flour
	½ teaspoon baking soda
⅓ cup milk	1 tablespoon tepid water

Follow directions for plain Crumpets (above), adding the orange juice and orange zest with the milk. *Makes 10.* ✹

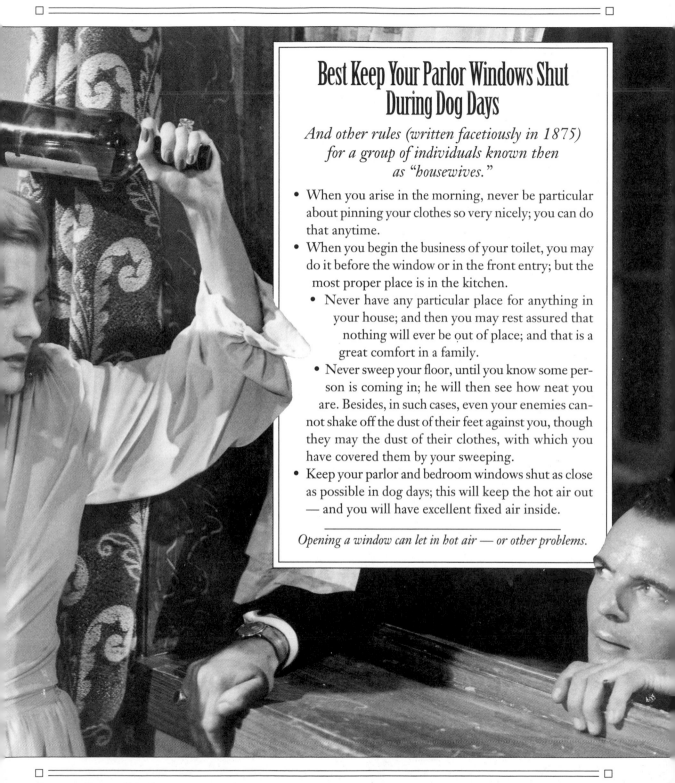

Best Keep Your Parlor Windows Shut During Dog Days

And other rules (written facetiously in 1875) for a group of individuals known then as "housewives."

- When you arise in the morning, never be particular about pinning your clothes so very nicely; you can do that anytime.
- When you begin the business of your toilet, you may do it before the window or in the front entry; but the most proper place is in the kitchen.
  - Never have any particular place for anything in your house; and then you may rest assured that nothing will ever be out of place; and that is a great comfort in a family.
  - Never sweep your floor, until you know some person is coming in; he will then see how neat you are. Besides, in such cases, even your enemies cannot shake off the dust of their feet against you, though they may the dust of their clothes, with which you have covered them by your sweeping.
- Keep your parlor and bedroom windows shut as close as possible in dog days; this will keep the hot air out — and you will have excellent fixed air inside.

Opening a window can let in hot air — or other problems.

The Superior Way to Crack
Hard-Shell Nuts

For formal social occasions, always do it before putting them on display for your guests. The reason will become obvious as you read these instructions . . .

EVERY NOW AND THEN, in one of our magazines, I see advertised a nut-cracking device resurrected from the past, refurbished and repolished. No doubt it will be eagerly seized upon by a new generation. I have used most of them, but to date I have not found any better device than a hammer, so I continue to use one. Cracking nuts with a hammer is an art. You will not become an expert overnight; the technique requires considerable experience and practice. Over the years, I have learned how to bring out halves in hickories, black walnuts, and butternuts almost every time — but I started cracking them some seventy years ago and have had a lot of practice.

Let's take a butternut. First of all, you remove the outer shell after it has become well dried out. You will then notice that one end of the nut is more pointed than the other. Stand the nut so that the more pointed end rests in a small depression (a cement block with a small gouge in it is excellent for this purpose). Naturally, you will be cracking the nuts someplace where the problem of shells does not have to be considered.

Now start tapping the blunt end with the hammer — not too hard at first, until you get the sound and feel of it. Don't be hasty! It should not crack before at least four or five taps, and often as many as a dozen are necessary. A hard bash, and you'll end up with crushed nutmeat. Each individual butternut is different in the texture and strength of its shell, so each one has to be treated separately. Properly tapped, the nut will break so the two meat halves easily come out of their intricate structures.

You use the same procedure for black walnuts. Here again, you will find one end more pointed than the other. Keep the pointed end down.

Hickory nuts are something else again. You definitely do not set them on end. Notice that although each hickory is different in size and shape, generally one edge is a bit more rounded than the other. You set the more pointed edge down in the same depression you used for the butternuts and start the same tapping procedure, this time along the edge of the nut. In all cases, make sure the flat of the hammer hits at right angles to the point of contact; otherwise the nut will break lopsided.

A hickory nut shell is much more flexible than the shell of a walnut or butternut. There is a spring to it when tapped with a hammer. (You definitely have to get the feel of it.) Your goal in cracking a hickory is not only to split it edgewise but also to so weaken the ends of the shell that they can be removed by pulling them away from the center part of the nut. Many times when the ends can be so withdrawn, you can come out with the complete whole nut, not merely the halves. Bringing them out in halves four times out of ten rates you a B.A.; getting them out in halves eight times out of ten rates you an M.A.; averaging nine out of ten for halves and one out of ten for a whole earns you a Ph.D.

I do not understand the technical mechanics involved, but I believe that the carefully controlled impact of the tapping gradually weakens and fractures the shell so that when it finally breaks, it does so along cleavage planes that permit the nutmeat to be easily extracted. Also, I think the proper drying of the nuts has something to do with it. I rarely try to crack a nut that has not dried for at least a year in some cool place, generally in a cellar. This year, I finished cracking the last of a batch of black walnuts gathered in Baiting Hollow, Long Island, five years ago. All the nutmeats were perfect.

Courtesy of Walter F. Wolf ✳

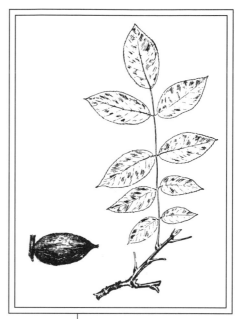

It takes about a dozen taps to open a butternut (top). *Hickory nuts* (above) *are trickier.*

Notes on A Coal Fire

As many Almanac readers discovered during the 1970s (this was featured in the 1976 edition), your living room or parlor fireplace doesn't need to be of the wood-burning variety . . .

By Marie E. MacIntyre

MY FAMILY'S EXPERIENCES with coal fires began one November day last year. I had recently returned from my annual pilgrimage to the United Kingdom and had brought home a toasting fork. Father appeared from behind the furnace with a 1910 black iron (now rusty) coal grate, which had elegantly graced some fireplace in the past. A minor bit of welding was required, costing about $10. A wire-brushing and some black stove paint restored the grate to more than a useful museum piece — it was an item anyone would be proud to possess.

BUYING A COAL GRATE

Our coal grate is a Victorian masterpiece. The best coal grate construction is of a deep basket type with close-fitting grates; the grate itself should stand about three inches off the floor. The closeness of the grates prevents small lumps of coal from falling through onto the hearth. The importance of height is really twofold — to get enough oxygen fed to the fire to keep it going well (draft) and to provide a place for the ashes, so that you do not have to shovel them more than once a month or so.

FINDING THE COAL YARD

After searching through the yellow pages, we were able to find a coal yard only a town away. We took all our plastic trash cans (in our house, we now use the older term *ashcans*, for obvious reasons!) to the coal yard. First, the car was weighed with us in it, but without the coal, on a wooden plank scale. Then we shoveled the coal into our ashcans, drove back to the scale, and reweighed the car. We had gained 275 pounds; the cost was about $3.50. Father thought that this was a bit high, since thirty-five years ago he had bought coal at $12.50 a ton!

It should be mentioned that we are talking about fireplace (or semibituminous) coal, and not anthracite, which is used for furnaces. In fact, I cannot stress too much the fact that you must get the right coal. The hard coal that is used in furnaces is similar to gravel in size and will not burn with the lush flame of the large, soft coal.

BUILDING THE FIRE

A coal fire is extremely easy to build. We have found that you can use the remains of leftover coal and add newspaper or other paper with a handful of kindling about eight inches long.

After stirring the coals with a poker to allow the dust to fall through the grate, you place the paper and the small bits of wood kindling on top of any remaining coal. Then add no more than six to eight pieces of coal to get the fire going. When the flames start up between the pieces of coal, more coal can be added to build a mound. Once the fire is going, a lump or two

Always leave home
with a tender good-bye
and loving words.
They may be the last..

– 1887 –

On the Subject of Fireplace Wood

*It's difficult to determine what's best. But the worst?
That's easy . . .*

BY CASTLE FREEMAN

FIFTEEN OR TWENTY years ago, when you couldn't vote in the state of Vermont unless you heated your house with wood, no intelligent adult was without an opinion on what was the best firewood. Oak, beech, and the rest each had its legion of proponents: one or another of them burned hotter, burned longer, made more coals.

I was never so certain myself. It seemed to me that the best wood came from the tree that grew closest to the woodshed. In an age of faith where firewood was concerned, I was an agnostic.

Since then, the debate seems sometimes to have become as quaint as that over the relative merits of the barouche and the hansom. I still burn my share, however, and I find, now that conviction is irrelevant, that I have entered upon a certainty with respect to firewood—not as to which is the best wood, but which is the worst. The worst firewood is butternut.

It doesn't look like lousy wood. The butternut is a substantial, broad-leaved tree with beautiful, pale brown wood having a perfectly respectable weight — when freshly cut, that is. Let that wood dry, though, and the same husky chunk of butternut that you heaved onto the stack when it was green now feels like a piece of foam. In a fire, it burns like a match and then disappears, leaving half a cup of cold and worthless powder. You might as well try to heat your house by putting a handful of cigarettes into your stove as to burn butternut. Fortunately, I have at least a year's supply.

added at intervals of two to three hours will keep a warm and attractive fire.

Through experience, we have found it best not to add coal if you are going to bed in an hour or so. Also, it's wise to close down the damper to the first notch so that the fumes can escape while maximum heat is retained.

THINGS YOU NEED

We were elated as we clustered around our first coal fire. Soon "Whatever happened to" questions were asked, such as "Whatever happened to the coal bucket?"

Mother remembered that it had been placed outside in the garden shed. We found it, swept away the cobwebs, and brushed, scraped, and painted it. It was a self-respecting coal bucket once again.

"Whatever happened to the coal shovel?" was heard at another fire session. Mother remembered that it was in a cupboard out on the porch. It, too, was brushed off, painted, and restored to usefulness. Eventually, a complete fireside ensemble was found almost intact in a house that had never had a coal fire!

If you have a toasting fork, you are all set. If not, use your barbecue forks. If you have never toasted muffins, hot dogs, or marshmallows on your own coal fire, the joys will enchant you. And you'll find many a cozy, cheery winter evening ahead. ✱

From 1853, a Rule to Be Taken Quite Seriously...

THE PERFECT HOSTESS will see to it that the works of male and female authors be properly separated on her bookshelves. Their proximity, unless they happen to be married, should not be tolerated.

Famous Last Words

(ALL TRUE)

The common thread is a lack of sorrow, an absence of horror. In fact, last words are often something pleasant to recall during the subsequent gathering of family and friends in the parlor . . .

COLLECTED BY BOB QUARTERONI

ALTHOUGH IT MAY SEEM morbid to some people, the collecting of last words is actually a very soothing occupation. As author Barnaby Conrad said, "After reading thousands of deathbed utterances, one is struck and comforted by how comparatively pleasant dying is reported to be. Especially when compared with other ordeals. Such as living, for example."

Indeed, one common thread that seems to bind many last words together is a strange lack of sorrow, an absence of horror. For example:

- Maria Mitchell, the first woman astronomer in America and a Nantucket native: "Well, if this is dying, there is nothing unpleasant about it."

- Near death, one Dr. Fidge, a foresighted man who had had a boat converted into a coffin and stored under his bed, suggested to his nurse: "Just pull my legs straight, and place me as a dead man; it will save you trouble shortly." And then he died.

- Clifton Fadiman once recalled a letter from a friend who wrote that when his father was dying, the nurse put her ear down close to the patient's face to see whether she could detect any breathing. The old gentleman opened his eyes and said, "Boo!"

- Henry David Thoreau, when he lay dying in 1862, was asked by a bedside companion if he had made his peace with God. Thoreau replied calmly that he was not aware of ever having quarreled with God. Then he uttered two enigmatic last words: "Moose . . . Indian . . ."

- When Ethan Allen, leader of the Green Mountain Boys, was dying, a parson told Allen that a band of angels was waiting. Allen answered, "Waiting are they? Waiting are they? Well, Goddam 'em, let 'em wait!"

- Carl Panzram, who murdered twenty-three people: "I wish the whole human race had one neck and I had my hands around it."

- James Rodgers, executed in 1960, was asked if he had any last request as he stood before a firing squad. "Why, yes," he said. "I'd like a bulletproof vest."

- And William Palmer's last words, as he stepped on a gallows trap in 1856, were: "Are you sure it's safe?"

- When Henry Ward Beecher, the orator and preacher, was dying at age seventy-four, his doctor asked him how high he

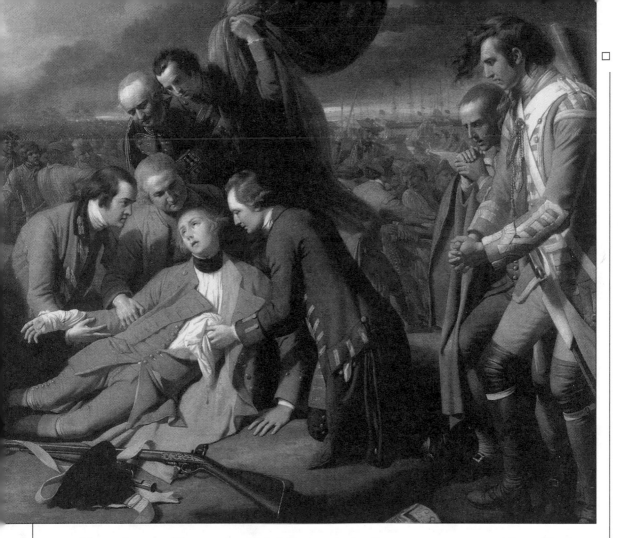

British General James Wolfe after conquering the French at Quebec: "Now I die contented."

could raise his arm. He replied, "Well, high enough to hit you, Doctor."

- Richard Monckton Milnes, a Victorian politician, uttered this deathbed quip: "My exit is the result of too many entrées."

ONE of the reasons people get interested in last words is to find out what famous and wise people have said at the end of their lives. What have they learned? What can we learn from them?

- Rabelais uttered what I consider the greatest of all exit lines: "I am going to the great perhaps."
- And former boxer Max Baer's last words are the all-time scariest: "Oh, God, here I go!"

BUT for each weighty last phrase, there are dozens of mundane or humorous statements that I find edifying. It's nice to know that scholars and famous writers are human, too.

- Dominique Bouhours, a

philosopher and grammarian, was concerned with sentence structure as he faced death: "I am about to — or I am going to — die: either expression is used."

- Oscar Wilde called for champagne, saying, "I am dying, as I have lived, beyond my means." ⊛

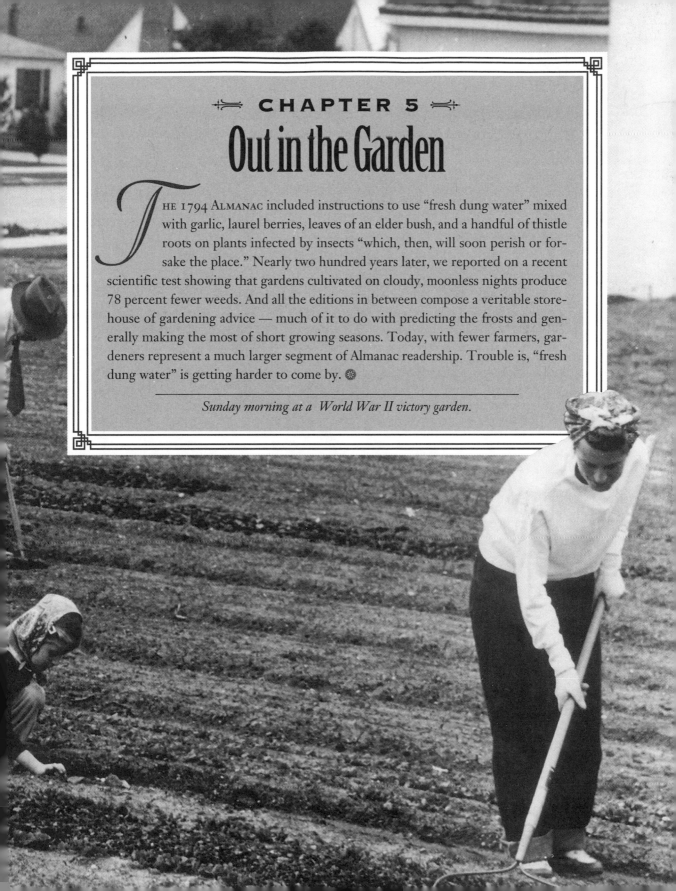

⟜ CHAPTER 5 ⟞
Out in the Garden

T HE 1794 ALMANAC included instructions to use "fresh dung water" mixed with garlic, laurel berries, leaves of an elder bush, and a handful of thistle roots on plants infected by insects "which, then, will soon perish or forsake the place." Nearly two hundred years later, we reported on a recent scientific test showing that gardens cultivated on cloudy, moonless nights produce 78 percent fewer weeds. And all the editions in between compose a veritable storehouse of gardening advice — much of it to do with predicting the frosts and generally making the most of short growing seasons. Today, with fewer farmers, gardeners represent a much larger segment of Almanac readership. Trouble is, "fresh dung water" is getting harder to come by. ◉

Sunday morning at a World War II victory garden.

How to Grow the Tastiest Tomatoes

You already know about watering, weeding, and feeding. Here's the real secret to superior taste.

By Roger A. Kline

The best tomatoes have always been large, soft, and runny — as in this 1918 ad for Campbell's soup.

A NY VEGETABLE gardening book worth its salt will describe the art of growing tomatoes. Choose rich soil, but not too rich in nitrogen or fresh manure. Plant after the last frost; choose a sunny location. Water, weed, feed, water, weed, and harvest. Pick them green if a frost threatens. In their haste to instruct you and move you on to the next vegetable, most garden books fail to explain some of the principles of flavor in tomatoes. It is important for gardeners to understand how a tomato can become the quintessence of a fine garden.

Flavor in tomatoes is a balance between sugars and acids. Individual taste prefers that the balance shift one way or the other. Added to this are the

"volatiles" — subtle chemical compounds that are very important for that full tomato flavor. Volatiles that have an off taste or aftertaste can ruin the perceived flavor. We will accept rough, misshapen, or even ugly fruits as long as they have a rich, appealing tomato flavor.

A major factor in the development of tomato flavor is the amount of leaf area exposed to the sun and the amount of sunlight that radiates on the plant. Consequently, small plant types with heavy fruit loads offer less flavor. Seasons that are rainy and overcast produce poor flavor compared with that of the same varieties grown under sunny conditions. Think of the leaves as factories that supply flavor compounds. The leaves are dependent on sunlight to manufacture these compounds; the leaves then distribute the compounds to the fruits. Therefore, the more leaves present, the more flavor compounds are produced and supplied to the tomatoes. Or, the fewer tomatoes on the plant with the same total leaf area, the more flavor is distributed to each individual tomato.

During a rainy season, the fruit set on any variety will be the same as in a sunny season. But because sunlight is needed to produce flavor compounds, those compounds are reduced during a cloudy season, and the same number of tomatoes must divide up fewer flavor units. The result is less flavor and lower quality.

There's not much you can do to increase the amount of sunlight in a growing season. But certain cultural practices affect the flavor of your tomatoes. Severe pruning, which some gardeners do when tomato plants are staked with a single main stem, drastically reduces the leaf tissue area, the site of manufacture of sugars and other compounds. This denies flavor units to the existing fruit load on a plant.

However, light pruning can increase the size of the fruits because of the redistribution of compounds away from the meristems (the technical term for certain formative tissues, or growing points) and to the fruits. Not only will the tomatoes be larger, but they also will mature earlier. Pruning does have certain drawbacks, sometimes causing problems with wilt, cracking, and

> Many flowers are good fried or frittered. Blossoms of squash, pumpkin, honey locust, day lily, elderberry, and yucca are all tasty. Yucca flowers are also delicious stir-fried with green peppers and garlic.
>
> – 1930 –
> **HOMER STILLSON**

blossom end rot, but research has shown that light pruning is a good practice, especially in large plant types with luxurious foliage.

Early types of tomatoes usually set fruits when the plant is young and small. These plants have less leaf area per tomato and do not have time to accumulate sugars. Therefore, early tomato types tend to have less flavor than late-season varieties.

Tomatoes enjoy warm weather, but it is said that in the South, they grow too fast to develop the sugars, acids, and beneficial volatiles needed for the best flavor.

Lifting plants up off the ground is a good way to avoid bruising and rotting, which can occur more easily if the fruits are in contact with the soil. Caging the plants without pruning them is a safe alternative to staking and trimming tomatoes. The cage should be large enough so the leaves are not pressed together but can intercept the sun as much as possible.

A tomato is not considered mature until it has developed gelatinous material around its seeds; the flavor compounds, as well as the vitamin C, are concentrated in this gel. Development of the gel occurs at temperatures above 60°F as the tomato begins to turn red. Supermarket tomatoes bred for shipping are picked before the gel develops; they usually lack flavor.

A tomato can even vary in flavor from one end to the other. Color change usually begins at the blossom end and proceeds toward the stem end. If you are very observant, you may see ripening occurring over the septa (inner walls) and then moving to the locule (open inner space containing the gel).

If you bite into a tomato and nothing oozes out, chances are the tomato lacks flavor. At the other end of the spectrum, Beefsteak tomatoes grown and ripened in the garden are embarrassingly sloppy to eat but have the best of all flavors. Tomatoes that are large, soft, and runny — those for which you must wear a bib, those you must eat in the privacy of your own home — are the greatest reward for the gardener. ✳

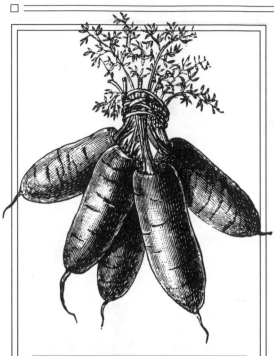

READERS' IDEAS

Planting & Pests

- Carrot, parsnip, and beet seeds must be planted very shallowly. Sift a thin layer of peat moss over the seeds, and the fragile seedlings will emerge readily.
  — Janeice Meier, Portland, Oregon

- Every year my spinach bolts before I get two meals. Last year, by accident, I planted the spinach close to the zucchini. The zucchini leaves grew and shaded the spinach. I had many meals after that happy accident!
  — Karen Larson
  Pittsburgh, Pennsylvania

- The old-fashioned way of ridding flowers of pests and insects was to grow castor-oil plants among roses and flowers. *— Ida Blaker*
  Ocean Grove, New Jersey

Dealing with Your Unsplittables

They're not as useless as you once may have thought . . .

By Castle Freeman

WELL, THE WOOD is in; the shed is full. The long stacks are built, filled, and braced. The ax, the maul, the steel wedges, and the heavy hammer are put away in their corner. The yard is picked up and raked. And inevitably, standing around the woodshed in no order, in silent reproach, are a couple of dozen chunks that could not be made to see the light: the unsplittables.

Unsplittables are crotch-bottom pieces, mostly, or they are pieces where a branch started or where the wood to be split was twisted or grew in a curve. Not all such pieces are unsplittable, however, and so a rebellious chunk is apt to announce itself only in that arresting moment when you strike the billet a mighty blow and your ax or maul bounces off the wood like a tennis ball dropped on a granite step. At that point, you may hit a couple of more licks, possibly turning the piece over. You can bring out the sledgehammer and wedges, but beware: unsplittables swallow steel wedges the way quicksand swallows dachshunds — without effect from the point of view of the quicksand and with utter finality from the point of view of the dachshund.

At this point, you are best advised to approach your unsplittables in the Way of the East: struggle no more, accept, embrace. That incorrigible block is not a useless unsplittable; it is a yule log, which will light your hearth next Christmas. I myself have a supply of yule logs that will take me through Christmas 2011. You may not need that many, but there are other paths out of the frustrating battlefield where you and the unsplittables vainly contend. Unsplittables make step stools and doorsteps. You can paint them white and use them to mark your driveway. You can furtively lose them beside back roads late at night. What you cannot do is split them.

The Case for Weeding in the Dark

*Sounds crazy, but a recent test in Germany has shown
that gardens cultivated on cloudy, moonless nights
produce 78 percent fewer weeds!*

By Jon Vara

WHERE DO ALL THOSE garden weeds come from? They come from seeds — seeds that, in most cases, are an integral part of the garden itself.

Microscopic scrutiny of a sample of fertile garden soil inevitably turns up a disheartening number of unwanted seeds — the product of generations of weeds that have grown, matured, died, and been incorporated into the soil. A single pigweed plant, for example, may produce several million seeds.

Moreover, buried weed seeds may remain viable for the better part of a century. During that time, they lie dormant and await conditions that will allow them to germinate, grow to maturity, and produce seeds of their own. Those conditions include relatively warm temperatures, adequate soil moisture, and — according to recent research by German botanists — exposure to light.

According to the German study — as reported in the journal *Die Naturwissenschaften* — the seeds of most common field weeds contain chemical triggers called phytochromes, which induce germination only when stimulated by light. Very brief flashes of light — lasting only a few thousandths of a second — will cause germination, even if the briefly exposed seeds are immediately reburied (as is likely to be the case during plowing, harrowing, sowing, and other soil-disturbing activities).

That is not particularly startling news in itself. As every experienced gardener knows, tilling the soil before planting also promotes weed growth, and attacking the initial weed crop with a hoe a few weeks later lays the groundwork for a successive crop of weeds.

What is intriguing about the German study is its suggestion of a novel approach to breaking the cycle of soil disturbance, light exposure, and weed growth. Rather than seeking to avoid disturbing the soil — as modern agribusiness does by replacing mechanical cultivation with chemical herbicide sprays or in some cases by no-till planting — the researchers tried eliminating the germination-inducing light. The results, they found, were "quite astonishing."

By performing all soil-disturbing operations after dark, they discovered that weed germination could be reduced by as much as 78 percent. Weeds typically covered only 2 percent of night-cultivated test strips, whereas adjacent strips cultivated during daylight hours were 80 percent covered with weeds.

Apparently, even the odd twinkle of starlight can be enough to activate some seeds. The researchers found that weed suppression was most pro-

OPPOSITE: *This lady may not get the results she expects. For the fewest weeds, it's best to garden without any light from the moon or stars.*

Gardeners will be interested to note that there is a 7.4-day cycle in the ability of bean seeds to take up water. Peaks in water uptake occur at new moon, full moon, and intervening quarters.

– 1976 –

Vegetable Magic

- When planting pepper plants, put a matchbook (without covers and staple) in the bottom of the planting hole. This encourages stronger, healthier plants.

  — *Nadine Salmons, Elbert, Colorado*

- When planting acid-loving plants such as peppers and eggplant, try a pinch of Epsom salts in the hole. The magnesium helps set blossoms; the sulfur adds acid.

  — *David Schaefer, Concord, Massachusetts*

- For the best-tasting tomatoes you ever ate, pour a cup of beer around the roots of each plant after it blossoms. Repeat once a week until the tomatoes are ripe.

  — *Reva Cobb, Spokane, Washington*

nounced when cultivation took place on cloudy, moonless nights. Light from artificial sources — such as headlight beams — also was enough to stimulate weed-seed germination. To prevent such unwanted exposure, tractor drivers participating in the study used sophisticated infrared night-vision equipment to maneuver across the fields in near-total darkness.

Few home gardeners will want to go to such extremes. Still, significant reductions in weed growth may be obtained by performing soil-disturbing operations on moonlit nights or at dawn or dusk.

For best results, the German researchers say, the soil preparation before crops are planted — plowing, harrowing, and other tillage — should be performed near noon on a bright sunny day. That will help to draw down the so-called seed bank by stimulating a large initial flush of weeds. Four weeks later, the immature weeds may be destroyed by nighttime cultivation, followed by nighttime seeding of crops.

A WORD OF CAUTION

The authors of the study suggest that it may be prudent to practice night cultivation only in alternate years. Although the vast majority of the millions of weed seeds slumbering in the soil will require the stimulus of light to germinate, a few light-independent renegades are inevitably present. If these dark germinators are allowed to mature and produce seeds of their own, the resulting progeny are likely to inherit the trait as well. After a few generations of such unintentional — and unwanted — selective pressure, the seed bank could become permeated with light-independent weed seeds, robbing nighttime cultivation of its effectiveness. ✳

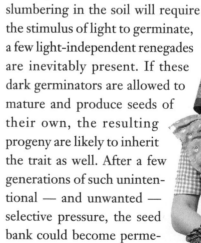

Keeping Raccoons Out of the Garden

None of the well-known tricks really works. So . . .

BY CASTLE FREEMAN

EVERY GARDENER who plants a sweet corn patch in the spring knows the raccoons are watching from the woods. Now August has come, the corn is ripe, and we are ready to eat it. The raccoons are ready, too.

If you decide to pick corn for your dinner on Tuesday, the raccoons will show up Monday night. They will eat it all, every ear, just when the corn is at its best. Many animals are smart, but the raccoon is both smart and patient. He will wait until the corn is ready, just as you do.

You may try all the common tricks for repelling raccoons. None of them works — or none of them works for long. Pie pans that rattle and bang, squash plants with prickly leaves, loud radios playing, rags soaked in kerosene, shaving cream on the fence posts, mothballs on the ground, blood meal, rubber snakes, plastic owls — no raccoon is going to be put off for very long by any of these. He may hold back for a night, but soon he'll understand that the pie pan and the kerosene are no real threat to him, and in he'll come. If you would keep him out, remember: the raccoon thinks the same way you do. He likes what you like (ripe sweet corn). He doesn't like what you don't like. Would a plastic owl repel you? No. Neither will it repel a raccoon.

You need a repellent that you know would work for you as well as for him. The Ayatollah Khomeini, say, or a well-armed member of the right wing fundamentalist group al-Jihad. No doubt those would be effective repellents, but they're complicated from the point of view of international restrictions on imports and exports. More practical repellents might be a vicious dog or a friend who likes to talk at length about investments, or television programs, or computers, or cars, or cameras. Either of these, stationed in your corn patch at night, will surely keep the raccoons away.

Remember that they like what you like.

Indoor Gardening Ideas for Kids

*From seeds and pits to Mr. Potato Face —
and the best part is that none of these projects requires
much parental guidance.*

By Lucille J. Goodyear

- **Common dried beans —** pole varieties such as navy, lima, and kidney — will produce fast-growing greenery. Soak the beans in water overnight, then plant them in moist, sandy soil. If you keep the soil damp, the sprouts will appear in a few days. When the plants begin trailing, they will wind around a support of some type. If not supported, they will trail down like ivy.

- **Another "quickie"** is a lentil garden. Line a shallow bowl with small pebbles, scatter a handful of lentil seeds over the pebbles, and fill the bowl with water. In two to four days, the child will have the beginning of an interesting cluster of greenery.

- **Citrus seeds** — grapefruit, orange, lemon, or lime — will usually sprout and grow into attractive little foliage plants. Presoak the seeds in warm water for a day or so in preparation for the planting. Then plant them in potting soil in clay pots and place them in a warm, semi-shaded spot until at least one pair of leaves sprout from each seed. Once these first leaves appear, you can bring the plants out to light and sunshine. Plants should be watered once a week — more often if the soil dries out rapidly. It is wise to have children plant a quick-growing project at the same time to keep their interest from waning while they're waiting for the citrus plants.

- **Avocado pits** can be grown in water or soil. If the pit is started in water, use a clear glass container so that the process can be readily observed. Whichever method you use, presoak the pit in water for a day, then peel the outer skin. Place the lower, pointed half of the pit in water. If it's too small to rest on the rim of a glass, insert a few toothpicks around the side of the pit to keep the upper, flat part clear of the water. You can let the plant continue to grow in the water or transfer it to a container of potting soil. (It's best to start several of these plants a few weeks apart to minimize the chance of disappointment.)

- **Carrot tops** growing in a shallow container of water make an interesting and amusing bit of greenery. Cut one-half inch from the top or leaf end of several carrots. Arrange them in a shallow dish with enough water barely to cover the bottoms of the carrot pieces at all times, while leaving the tops exposed. (Sand or small pebbles under the car-

rots will help you accomplish this.) Add water as it evaporates. Within a few days, the carrot tops will begin to show a growth of delicate, feathery green leaves.

- **The root end of celery** can be cut off and handled in the same manner as the carrot tops. It will grow taller than the carrot cuttings, and the two can be combined in the same container for a most attractive arrangement. (Another method of growing carrot or celery cuttings is to place them in a dish of sand or vermiculite kept moderately moist.)

- **Beet tops** also can be used in this type of planting. Because these plants grow rapidly, they are exciting and satisfying projects for young gardeners.

- Perhaps one of the fastest-growing plants is **the sweet potato.** Select a large, firm potato that has two or more "eyes" beginning to show a little purple or green growth. Suspend the potato, root end down, in a container of water, keeping the upper part dry. In a few days, the start of a root system will appear. If a long, trailing vine is desired, pinch off all but two or three leaf branches; if a bushier plant is desired, al-

low all the sprouts to grow. The sweet potato will also take root and sprout leaves when planted in sandy soil, if you make sure that all the "eyes" are covered. (This method takes a bit longer than the water method.)

- **A white potato** will allow you to be a bit more creative. Scoop some pulp from one end of a large potato and fill the hollow with wet cotton. Slice off the other end of the potato and place it in a shallow dish lined with pebbles and filled with water. Sprinkle grass seed over the moistened cotton, lodging it in place with the tip of a toothpick or pencil point. If the water level is kept so that the potato is constantly supplied with water, it will sprout a fine thatch of "green hair," which can be cut occasionally, if necessary, with tiny scissors. Use charcoal chips to form the eyes, nose, and mouth of "Mr. Potato Face!" ❀

The Very Best Kind of Snow Shovel

It may not even be a snow shovel at all . . .

BY CASTLE FREEMAN

NOW, AS THE SEASON of storms approaches, a bewildering multiplicity of snow shovels has gone on display in practically every store in town. With winter coming, you can buy a snow shovel in a grocery store, a sporting-goods store, a drugstore. Snow shovels are hawked with special fervor at those curious hybrid establishments known as "home centers." (In more plain-spoken times, they were called "hardware stores" and "lumberyards.") And what snow shovels they are! There are snow shovels that look like shovels; there are others that look like really large dental tools. There are even snow shovels that look like Eskimo perambulators. There are snow shovels with straight handles, snow shovels with bent handles; with fat blades, with thin blades; with D grips, with T grips. Some snow shovels are plastic and cost a couple of bucks; others are so expensive that it seems wrong to expose them to a substance, like snow, that comes for free. What to do?

It took me a number of winters to discover that very often the best snow shovel is not a shovel at all. Get yourself a simple broom — one with long, stiff straw. A broom will take care of better than half the snow you'll get in a winter, and it won't break your back, burst your heart, or dig up your grass by mistake. For cleaning snow off the car, the broom is far superior to the shovel because it can't scratch your paint job. And if you are equipped with a broom and you should, at last, get a fall of snow too deep for your broom to overcome, you can simply hop on it and fly south until you get to a latitude where snow is unknown and the home centers sell only those shovels that come with pails for use at the beach.

A good broom is better.

Never, Never Go Down to the Cellar

But if you must, keep in mind these basic rules.

By Castle Freeman

NATURE MADE the cellars of old houses to be low, dark, dirty, and damp for a good reason: so people would keep out of them. We can come to no good end through disregarding the warnings of nature — ask anyone who lives in rattlesnake country. Or ask me. I have concluded, from more than one bitter lesson, that he who expects to do any good by entering his cellar plays water polo with crocodiles.

One day I discovered in my house a section of floor that felt soft — you know, springy? Better investigate, I thought. Opened the cellar door and descended, like Orpheus. Found in my own cellar a scene that Poe would have rejected as excessively macabre: dripping walls, gloom, dank cobwebs, dust, and a sorrowful air of profound decay. Looked for the underpinnings of the springy floor, but made no headway, owing to a lack of light. Went back upstairs for a light (my second mistake).

Returning to the cellar with the light, I soon found the problem: a busted floor joist. How did that happen? Is that joist maybe a trifle rotten? And, really, the one beside it looks a mite poorly itself. What about the beam? Oh, dear. Big job there. Expensive. And what's that over there? . . .

It is what you learn down there that is painful — far more painful than any repair you make can be satisfactory. I found three rotten sills, four leaking water pipes, a place where the foundation kind of bulges, and any number of holes in the walls. Therefore, that others may be spared, I announce the Three Theses of the Cellar, as follows: (1) Never go into your cellar. (2) If you must go into your cellar, never take a light. (3) If you must be in your cellar with a light, keep your eyes shut.

How to Weed Your Garden for Chicken Feed

Cleaning up the garden in the fall is a dirty, tedious job.
So this author brings in 14 very cheap helpers.

By Earle Barnhart

AT THE END of the growing season, a vegetable garden can look a little tattered — a few fallen cornstalks here, a flattened tomato vine there, a wilted pepper plant, maybe a few dried weeds.

The most important cleanup job is to pull up the stems and stalks of weeds. Every weed that had time to become mature probably produced seeds. A single dried stem can contain thousands of seeds, and each seed is a potential weed in your garden next year. The other important chore is to get rid of spoiled vegetables and crop stems in the rows, sometimes a messy business.

Because the work can be dirty and tedious, I don't do it myself. I have a crew of fourteen small but remarkably energetic workers. They work ten-hour days, every day. They don't speak English. They sleep huddled together in a single unheated room with no running water. They are Asian in origin. They're chickens.

They seem to enjoy their work thoroughly. They enter the fenced garden through a low chicken-wire tunnel that connects their house to the garden area. Each morning, they leave the chicken house and literally run to the garden to get started. During the day, they can move freely from their house to the garden and back.

THE JOB DESCRIPTION

An experienced garden chicken works to a set of firm priorities. The first task is to eat any damaged or over-ripe vegetables that remain unharvested in the garden. The next priority is to eat any weed seed or insect that is easy to find on the soil's surface. After that, tasty vegetable stalks are pecked apart and digested. Broccoli stems seem to be a favorite, as are carrot tops, chard, and kale. Intriguingly, they won't touch ripe eggplants or sage.

READERS' IDEAS

Fertilizer

A testing kit is the modern way
To find out what to add to your clay.
Old farmers need no kits or guess
For growing a garden with great
    success.
Their ancient sure-fire knowledge
    lives:
It's now called "barnyard additives."

— *Evan Burns*
South Hadley, Massachusetts

THE OLD FARMER'S ALMANAC BOOK OF EVERYDAY ADVICE

After surface demolition comes excavation, digging around any root or onion bulb for soil insects or unwary worms. Finally comes a period of general scratching that thoroughly mixes all the shredded organic matter into the top few inches of soil and levels it.

Although chickens are not particularly bright, they are impressively persistent. They consider every leaf, stem, and clod of soil as a target to be continually pecked and scratched, apparently in hopes of finding a tasty weed seed, worm, or bit of plant. These small but frequent rewards during the workday are a great motivation, a production-management technique used by many of today's most successful businesses.

THE BOTTOM LINE

In one week alone, I figure I get more than 980 chicken hours of highly specialized help. You try picking thousands of individual weed seeds out of your entire garden. Try digging, shredding, and blending into the soil all the plant residues from the summer. Finally, try converting dozens of insect pests into highly nutritious eggs on your midmorning break. I guarantee that you and your garden will benefit from the special talents of working chickens. ✺

Making the Most of Your Manure Pile

Like wine and men, no two manures are identical.

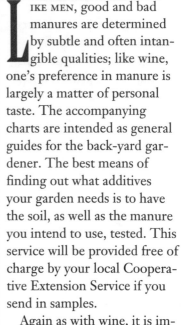

L IKE MEN, good and bad manures are determined by subtle and often intangible qualities; like wine, one's preference in manure is largely a matter of personal taste. The accompanying charts are intended as general guides for the back-yard gardener. The best means of finding out what additives your garden needs is to have the soil, as well as the manure you intend to use, tested. This service will be provided free of charge by your local Cooperative Extension Service if you send in samples.

Again as with wine, it is important how you store your manure. Manure is best kept in a pile, which makes it more likely to retain its nutrients and makes you less likely to accidentally step in it. The use of bedding (straw, sawdust,

or mulch hay) also will help in preventing nutrients from evaporating or leaching into the ground. Bedding, as it decomposes over time, will raise the organic matter content of your manure. This is particularly beneficial with poultry and rabbit manures, which have a high nutrient content

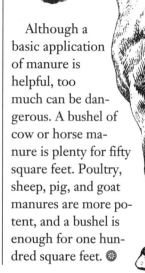

but are low in organic matter.

Most manures are best used in conjunction with a commercial fertilizer, which will provide the nutrients your manure may be lacking. A "complete" fertilizer — one that contains a percentage of each of the three key nutrients (nitrogen, phosphate, and potassium [potash]) — is preferred. The results of the testing samples will tell you how much of each to add. Chemical fertilizers are generally less expensive than manures, but they will not provide the organic matter essential to maintaining rich soil.

Although a basic application of manure is helpful, too much can be dangerous. A bushel of cow or horse manure is plenty for fifty square feet. Poultry, sheep, pig, and goat manures are more potent, and a bushel is enough for one hundred square feet.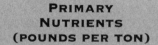

TYPE OF MANURE	WATER CONTENT	PRIMARY NUTRIENTS (POUNDS PER TON)		
		NITROGEN	PHOSPHATE	POTASH
Cow, horse	60%–80%	12–14	5–9	9–12
Sheep, pig, goat	65%–70%	10–21	7	13–19
Chicken				
Wet, sticky, caked	75%	30	20	10
Moist, crumbly to sticky	50%	40	40	20
Crumbly	30%	60	55	30
Dry	15%	90	70	40
Ashes	0%	0	135	100

TYPE OF GARDEN	BEST TYPE OF MANURE	BEST TIME TO APPLY
Flower	Cow, horse	Early spring
Vegetable	Chicken	Fall
	Cow, horse	Spring
Potato or other root crop	Cow, horse	Fall
Acid-loving plants	Cow, horse	Early fall or not at all
(blueberries, azaleas, mountain laurel, rhododendrons)		

PART TWO

Advice for Your Life

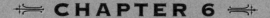

CHAPTER 6

Those Carefree Childhood Years

IN 1867, THE ALMANAC advised that every young boy ought to know how to harness a horse, plow a field, milk a cow, "reckon" money, whitewash a wall, and swing a scythe. In the same edition, a young girl was told she should be able to sew, sweep carpets, knit, make bread, write letters, nurse the sick (without fainting at the sight of blood), trim lamps, and entertain visitors. Obviously, childhood was not so "carefree" during the early days of the Almanac. It wasn't until this century that children were allowed to be children. So almost all the material in this chapter is taken from the past sixty to seventy years — a period of time that's broad enough to include some fond childhood memories for most of us. But have you noticed that, as we get older, our childhood seems to grow more carefree every time we think back on it? ❀

A spring day, three of your very best friends, and not a care in the world. Remember?

Some Good Ways to Find North Without a Compass

One involves your wristwatch; another, 2 stakes in the ground; many use stars, certain plants, and even animals.

BY DOUGALD MACDONALD

M Y SCOUTMASTER insisted I would never get lost if I looked for the moss that grows only on the north side of trees. Well, maybe, but it never worked for me; given enough shade and moisture, moss will grow just about anywhere. Such imprecision is typical of most of the so-called natural compasses heralded in survival manuals — but there are some that can be quite accurate, as well as fun to test.

For instance, you may notice that deciduous trees grow predominantly on the south side of hills, but conifers are usually found on the north. In the high Rockies, limber pines grow on the south and east sides of mountains; Engelmann spruce trees grow on the north. Plants often adapt to the existing conditions: trees grow fuller on the south side, and evergreens are usually bent away from the prevailing wind (if the wind is usually from the northwest, the treetops will grow to the southeast). In the desert, the giant barrel cactus always leans to the south. Such tendencies can indicate directions to a knowledgeable observer. The pilotweed, whose leaves grow in a north–south line, helped guide the first settlers across the Great Plains and became known as the "compass plant" of the prairies.

Other natural signs are supported less by empirical evidence than by long tradition. Spruce gum drawn from the south side of trees is said to have a clear, amber color, but that from the north side is soiled and grayish. Leonardo da Vinci was the first to report that the north side of most trees has thicker bark and wider growth rings to protect against chilly north winds. Spider webs can show direction, too. Given a choice, the theory goes, spiders will orient the web facing southeast to catch the morning sun. In practice, however, they can lay only the first thread with the wind, so most webs are parallel to the prevailing wind. Animals like a warm, sunny home as much as people do, and most birds' nests, squirrels' nests, and even anthills are found to the lee of the prevailing wind, often facing the sun.

> It is much better to know about the smallest vine twisting up the most remote canyon in the Rockies than to know the entire Grand Canyon in a glance.
>
> **JOAQUIN MILLER**

THE OLD FARMER'S ALMANAC BOOK OF EVERYDAY ADVICE

The sun was probably people's first natural guide. At noon, it lies due south every day of the year. It is a mistake, however, to assume that the sun rises in the east and sets in the west. It does approximately, of course, but depending on your latitude, the shape of the horizon, and the time of year, sunrise and sunset may be as much as forty degrees off the cardinal points. The moon, too, reaches its highest point above the horizon at due south, but this can be predicted conveniently only once a month — exactly at midnight at full moon.

It is easy to find north within just a few degrees by tracing the movement of shadows. At midmorning, anytime from 8:30 to 11:00 A.M., drive a stake into the ground and

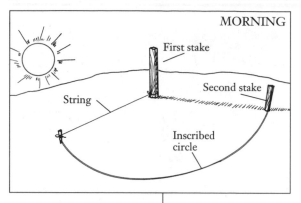

MORNING

First stake

Second stake

String

Inscribed circle

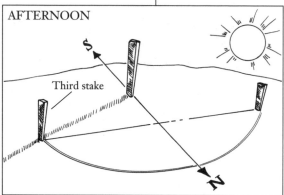

AFTERNOON

S

Third stake

N

All you need to find north is a piece of string and three stakes (see text). Or, as below, a wooden match and a wristwatch. Once north is found, then the challenge is to find home.

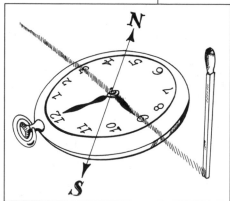

N

S

mark the end of its shadow with another stake. Tie a string to the first stake and, using the distance between the two stakes as the radius, inscribe a circle in the dirt around the original stake. As the sun gets higher, the shadow will fall within the circle. After noon, the shadow will grow longer; with a third stake, mark the point where it hits the circle again. Now measure the distance between the two points on the circle and locate the middle (try taking the distance with the string and halving it). The midpoint and the original stake will be the endpoints of a north–south line.

Another method, which sacrifices some accuracy but takes only a few minutes, uses a wristwatch. Place the watch on a level surface and hold a match or small stick upright against its edge — a thin enough object will cast a faint shadow even on overcast days. Now turn the watch slowly until the stick's shadow is aligned with the hour hand. A line drawn from the center to a point halfway between the hour hand and twelve o'clock on the dial will point south.

On a clear night, you can use the stars to find directions by tracing their relative movements. Drive a stake at eye level in an open clearing. Drive another, taller stake behind it, so the two tips line up on a bright star. After a few minutes, the star will seem to have moved across the sky (the stars only *seem* to move, of course, as the earth rotates beneath them). The apparent movement indicates the direction you are facing. If your star moves up, you are facing east; if it moves down, you're facing west; right means south; left means north.

Of all the natural direction finders, only one is truly reliable. The North Star, Polaris, lies directly over the North Pole. You can find it by connecting the two stars marking the end of the familiar Big Dipper and tracing a line across the sky to the next bright star — about the distance from your outstretched thumb to your middle finger held at arm's length. Long before the compass was invented, before magnetism had been discovered, mariners were navigating by the North Star. It moves only slightly during the year and thus is by far the most accurate of nature's beacons. ✸

How to Tell Time by the Stars

By Edward Barnatowics

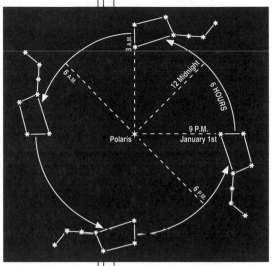

BEFORE THE ADVENT of the modern clock, the time of day was determined by the position of the sun. But did you ever wonder how our ancestors stayed on schedule after the sun went down? They told time simply by looking at the stars.

You can do the same, but to use our "star clock," you have to be able to identify the Big Dipper (Ursa Major), whose two Pointers (Merak and Dubhe) are used to locate the North Star (Polaris).

Now the Big Dipper is a circumpolar constellation, which means that for anyone north of forty-one degrees latitude, it never rises or sets. It just keeps revolving around Polaris, making a little more than one revolution a day.

An imaginary line that connects the two pointers and Polaris makes up the single hand of our star clock. If our single hand swings completely around Polaris in twenty-four hours, it follows that if our hand rotated through ninety degrees (one-quarter of a revolution), six hours would have passed (one-quarter of twenty-four hours is six hours).

As an example, the diagram illustrates the position of the Big Dipper on January 1 about 9 P.M. Using this six-hour quarter circle as a convenient increment, we can further increase our accuracy. For example, if our hand rotated through forty-five degrees from its 9 P.M. position, it would be three hours later, or twelve midnight.

With some practice, you'll surprise yourself at being able to tell time to within fifteen minutes! And if you're a stickler for accuracy, you might be interested to know that humans have yet to develop a timepiece as accurate as the apparent movement of the stars. In fact, the world's most accurate clocks are checked by star time.

After the sun goes down, a "star clock" can be accurate to within fifteen minutes. To use it, you must be able to locate the North Star and the Big Dipper.

The Secrets Behind
Famous Old Magic Tricks

*Some (but not all) of these are pretty
easy to do . . .*

MAKE A CARD PASS FROM ONE PACK TO ANOTHER

THE PERFORMER takes two extra aces — one of spades, one of hearts. He cuts the mark of the spade out carefully and does the same with the heart. He places a little soap on the back of each cutout mark, then lays the spade cutout over the heart ace and the heart cutout over the spade ace. Each (now counterfeit) ace is then placed on the bottom of one half of the pack. After showing his audience the counterfeit aces, the performer surreptitiously rubs off the soaped-on marks and again shows the cards to the audience — who, of course, will perceive the cards to have changed packs. The secret consists in the magician stamping his foot or making some other distraction so the audience doesn't catch him slipping off the marks.

MAGIC BOTTLE

The magician takes a small bottle, the neck of which is not over one-sixth inch in diameter. Using a funnel, she fills this bottle with red wine. She places the bottle in a glass container that's about two inches taller than the bottle, then fills this glass vessel with water. Gradually, the water will replace the wine in the small bottle. The reason: Water, which is specifically heavier than wine, must hold the lower place.

SEEING THINGS

The concave mirror is the staple instrument of any magician's cabinet. Many weird effects may be (and have been) obtained from such. In the drawing, a large concave mirror (A) has been placed in an apartment separate from the one where the spectator stands. A small inverted object (as white as possible) is placed at B. A strong light, also hidden from view, is thrown upon this object. A spectator at point D will see an erect image of the object, suspended in the air in the open frame (C). Other spectators standing at a little distance on either side of the first, however, will not see it. ✹

Like many sleight-of-hand tricks, the concave mirror illusion is simpler to explain than to perform successfully.

Rope Skipping Across America

Just as predictable as the arrival of spring is the appearance of children skipping rope and reciting rhymes that are often unique to their particular region of the country.

By Francelia Butler

WHEN THE WEATHER becomes not too warm, not too cold, as if by magic, it signals children to get out their jump ropes and begin to skip and chant. Each spring, this phenomenon is as predictable as the cycles of the moon.

"I can do the rumba," the verse went. "I can do the split. I can turn around and show my slip!" Clearly, the women's movement hadn't arrived yet.

Some ancient sketches show men as the skippers, and one antique Greek vase shows a maiden skipping a grapevine instead of a rope. Some scholars believe that the skipping was a ritual to make the crops grow — the higher the skip, the taller the plants. Skipping is still clearly a ritual, a ceremony, for within the invisible world of the whirling rope, if children stumble, they start in again from the beginning. For the spell to work, it must be performed perfectly.

In the early nineteenth century, both boys and girls skipped, but the pastime came to be predominantly one for girls. The first rhymes chanted by American skippers were lyrical verses descending from English sources. Children being traditionalists, these rhymes passed from child to child and

Top time's gone,
kite time's come,
April Fools' Day will
soon be here.

18TH–19TH CENTURY
SAYING

still linger alongside their rough native counterparts. Here is a romantic English rhyme with an interesting history:

> On the hilltop stands a lady.
> Who she is I do not know.
> All she wears is gold and silver
> And she needs a nice young man.

I first heard this rhyme in 1945 on the playground of a school in Ball's Hill, Virginia, where it was preserved by the black culture. The rhyme is from an old English ballad, "O No, John!" of which there are many versions. I learned that the early American politician John Randolph of Roanoke knew some of the lines in his early childhood and, years later, wrote to a friend asking for the rest. It had been taught him, he recalled, "by a mulatto servant girl." The rhyme can now be found in New England, the Midwest, and the West, as well as in the South.

From one generation to another in the United States, rope skipping has always been popular. My late mother-in-law, born in 1861, skipped to the following folk rhyme, first in New York and then in Connecticut:

> Intry, mintry, cutry, corn
> Apple seed and apple thorn
> Wire brier, limber lock
> Three geese in a flock
> One flew East and
> One flew West and
> One flew over the cuckoo's nest!

My mother-in-law remembered that at about the same time she learned the rhyme, she was spanked for mussing her great-grandmother's black shawl — which was tied to the doorknob in mourning for President Lincoln!

Unlike many European rhymes used for skipping, American rhymes tend to be lively and spunky, expressing problems and suggesting solutions. This East Coast protest rhyme is an example:

> I won't go to Macy's anymore, more, more
> There's a big fat policeman at the door, door, door.
> He took me by the collar and he made me pay a dollar
> So I won't go to Macy's anymore, more, more!

No doubt the reader will recall hearing some of these rhymes in other areas. America is a mobile society, and as children move, they carry their

(continued on page 118)

Make Your Echo Answer Questions

Echoes are fun — and they're even more so when used to answer a question by echoing the last word of the question — for example, "What are they who pay three guineas/To hear a tune of Paganini's?" The echo will seem to answer, "Pack o' ninnies." Or how about Dean Swift's lines:

"What must we do our Passion to express?" (Echo — "press.")
"Say what can keep her chaste whom I adore?" (Echo — "a door.")
"Is there no way to moderate her anger?" (Echo — "hang her.")

The hills were alive with echoes in The Sound of Music.

rhymes with them. Among the rhymes that are popular all over the Unite
States is this "death" rhyme:

> Mother, Mother, I am ill.
> Call for the doctor over the hill.
> Doctor, doctor, will I die?
> Yes, my dear, and so will I.

By far the most popular rhyme in the United States is "Teddy Bea
— a rhyme now heard in variations around the world. It seems to date from
the presidency of Theodore Roosevelt.

> Teddy bear, teddy bear,
> Turn around.
> Teddy bear, teddy bear,
> Touch the ground.
> Teddy bear, teddy bear,
> Shine your shoe.
> Teddy bear, teddy bear,
> That will do.

Many "love" rhymes have tra
eled all around the country:

> Elvis Presley,
> How about a date?
> Meet you at seven
> Or half past eight.
> I can do the rumba.
> I can do the split.
> I can turn around
> And show my slip.

Rope-skipping rhymes are
many and varied as seashells, a
many skippers will recall oth
rhymes and childhood experien
connected with them. Next spri
when the trees begin to bud, p
haps you'll be able to add to yo
own collection. Just listen to t
children . . . ❈

Fashioning a Willow Whistle

SOME BOYS STILL PLAY marbles; a few go fishing. But somewhere along the years, they have lost the "feel" of spring. They aren't equipped for it. How many boys today have a jackknife — for cutting an alder pole, making a slingshot or kite, or whittling a shingle boat? Or especially, and most important, fashioning a willow whistle?

That was the supreme accomplishment. First you'd cut a willow twig about six inches long. You'd notch halfway through the small end, then tap the twig gently all around with the knife till the bark loosened and could be slipped off. Next, for the whistle top, you'd whittle a flat surface between the notch and the mouthpiece. Only then would you slip the bark back on, setting it up so the notches matched. After making a slanting cut on the underside of the mouth end, you were ready to whistle — slipping the bark up and down to change pitch. You'd have a willow whistle — in truth the pipe of spring.

18 Rules for Good Riting

- Each pronoun agrees with their antecedent.
- Just between you and I, case is important.
- Verbs has to agree with their subjects.
- Watch out for irregular verbs which has cropped into our language.
- Don't use no double negatives.
- A writer mustn't shift your point of view.
- When dangling, don't use participles.
- Join clauses good, like a conjunction should.
- Don't use a run-on sentence you got to punctuate it.
- About sentence fragments.
- In letters themes reports articles and stuff like that we use commas to keep a string of items apart.
- Don't use commas, which aren't necessary.
- It's important to use apostrophe's right.
- Don't abbrev.
- Check to see if you any words out.
- In my opinion I think that an author when he is writing shouldn't get into the habit of making use of too many unnecessary words that he does not really need.
- And, of course, there's that old one: Never use a preposition to end a sentence with.
- Last but not least, lay off clichés.

Courtesy of Stan Schirmacher.

The Case for a Pet Cricket

They're easy to manage, they won't last very long, you'll love (or hate) their singing, they don't eat much . . . but beyond all that, there really are some interesting aspects to owning one of these lovable little creatures.

By Kathleen Kilgore

I'VE NEVER MET another American family that keeps pet crickets, although they are still prized in Japan and probably China. My mother got the idea from a 1925 kindergarten teacher's textbook.

A field cricket is shiny black, with brown wings. There are no green crickets — Hollywood's Jiminy Cricket to the contrary. A fully grown male is a bit less than an inch long, and the female is about 50 percent longer. They are easy to tell apart, and telling them apart is vital if you want one for a pet, because the female does not sing. At his rear, the male has two thin, pronglike sensory organs. The female has three prongs, the middle and longest one being her ovipositor, with which she injects eggs into the soil. A cricket is shorter and stubbier than a grasshopper and stays close to the ground. The cricket won't jump except in desperation.

In the fall, the female lays her eggs in the ground. They hatch in May or early June, producing thousands of tiny black crickets swarming in the tall grass. They molt rapidly, and by the time they are large enough to start singing in late July or early August, they have become not only bigger but also more cautious. The male selects a den to which he can retreat at a moment's notice — a tiny hole in the ground, a crack in a cement wall, a crevice under a piece of bark — and begins to sing.

Unlike the grasshopper, the cricket doesn't sing by rubbing his legs together. He lifts his wing casings at a 45-degree angle and rubs them together — the insides are lined with tiny sawtooth projections.

The cricket sings to attract a mate. But in captivity, he will also sing when you give him food (crickets can eat and sing at the same time). Some crickets become so tame they will sing when you blow gently on them — they seem to like the warmth. Like all insects, crickets are cold-blooded, and they sing faster or more slowly depending on the temperature.

From my own experiments, it seems that the cricket's song is territorial. One fall I recorded such a song on tape. When the recording was played across the room, the cricket showed no interest. But when I placed it near his cage, he went wild, clawing at the sides to get at his rival. After a few more tries, I determined his territory to be about two feet in diameter. In China, male crickets were made to fight like roosters by putting two at a time in a pottery jar. They will fight whether a female is present or not. And they fight fiercely, losing legs and antennae, often to the death.

So it's best not to keep two males in a cage. And don't take pity on your frustrated male and give him a female for company, unless you have kinky voyeuristic tastes. The female is much bigger, and in a cage, the male has no chance to escape. After their amour, you'll probably find Madame polishing off the remains of her lover.

I've experimented with several kinds of cages, jars, and fishbowls and found that the best cricket house is a medium-size pickle jar with holes punched in the lid. By far the worst home for a pet cricket is a cute sandalwood-and-bamboo cricket cage imported from Japan. The cricket squeezes himself between the bars or, failing that, simply chews through the bamboo.

After you get your cricket, you can add sand or clean soil and leaves to the bottom of his container. A piece of bark makes him feel more at home. If a pickle jar is out of place in your decorating scheme, you could put him in a fishbowl or terrarium. But the top must be covered tightly with wire mesh, and even with that, crickets can sometimes squeeze underneath the edge, or hurt themselves trying. You're safer with a ventilated screw top.

Now comes the hard part: the hunt. Crickets abound in fields and front lawns. But the minute you get within a few feet of a cricket, he shuts up and retreats into his hole. The best place to catch him is on your own turf. In the fall, crickets often come inside, attracted by the warmth. Anytime you hear one singing in a bathroom or cellar, you've found a potentially easy catch.

Once you have what you are pretty sure is a cricket in your hand, be careful. Their legs and antennae can break off, and they can bite like crazy. Your pickle jar is sitting on the shelf miles away, so the next best thing is a cotton handkerchief. Wrap the cricket loosely so that he won't suffocate, and try to get him home as soon as possible.

The best place to transfer the cricket to his jar is the bathtub. After he becomes tame, you can put him safely in another jar while you clean the old one — just tip his old jar, and he will slide down the glass. But a newly caught cricket will make desperate attempts to escape. Close the drain and shower curtain — a glass-enclosed shower stall is ideal.

Your cricket needs both food and water every day. For water, the most convenient dish is the lid of a plastic medicine jar. You can put it into the cricket's jar with tweezers and fill it by drawing water through a straw and then releasing it into the dish. The water dish should be cleaned and refilled every day. I had one cricket who used to sit in his water dish all day, but generally crickets just drink from it.

Crickets will eat almost anything, including your woolens, if they escape. They like cereals of all kinds: cornflakes, oats, granola. They are crazy about birdseed, especially sunflower seeds, and will also eat apple peelings, lettuce, raw carrots, and other raw vegetables. It's best to go easy on the food. They eat very little; any food that's not eaten should be removed every day so the jar won't grow mold. I usually clean the jar and put in fresh dirt every two or three days.

Now we come to the sad part. A cricket's life span is very short. In fact, this is one pet children will not get tired of before it goes. Outdoors, the first frost kills the crickets, but even in a warm house with good care, they don't winter over. If you catch one in good condition in August or September, he should last until Thanksgiving. But I have never had one make it to Christmas.

Sometimes you will just find the cricket lifeless in the morning. Sometimes they seem to lose their balance and flop about — when that happens, I put them outdoors where I can't see them. And occasionally you'll have a cricket whose song one night just gets fainter and fainter, like Tinker Bell in *Peter Pan*, until it fades away by dawn. Then dump the jar out on the lawn, give it a good washing, and put it away for next fall.

He that can't paint
must grind colors.

– 1865 –

A Lemonade Stand Story

By Castle Freeman

PEOPLE IN THE RETAIL business will tell you that the three secrets of keeping store are location, location, and location. But if you're a young entrepreneur just starting out, and if your premises are at all rural, you may have to learn the importance of location the hard way. The young entrepreneur I'm thinking of was six last August. Finding herself short of funds and wanting to celebrate summer by shining up one of the icons of American childhood, she decided to open a lemonade stand beside the road on which she lived. The lemonade she made, with a little help in directing the sugar toward the pitcher. A table, paper cups, ice, a sign, a money box, and the elements of commerce seemed all to be in place. On August 5, she opened for business. A nickel a cup was the price.

Location was not long in delivering its stern verdict. The road her stand served, while not entirely devoid of traffic, was about a four- or five-car-per-hour road on a Tuesday morning. The cars that did pass tended to be the same ones, moreover, and their drivers tended not to be thirsty. They'd wave, but they wouldn't buy. Beer crowd, I guess. In any case, business was not brisk. I bought a cup, and I stood the house one; but although my money was good, I'm a close relative of the proprietor, so my trade was not too important.

"Bit slow," I remarked.

"I'm never going to make any money," the proprietor said.

"Cheer up," I said. "Maybe a bus will come along, and you'll sell it all at once."

"Buses never come along," she said. I bought another cup.

"Can you watch for a while?" she asked.

"Me?" I said.

And so another small business became a statistic.

Only the young die good.

– 1905 –

The three secrets of business: location, location, location.

A Formula for Short-Range Weather Forecasts

You start with a boy and a turtle and then, well, read on . . .

SCOTT BROWN, MANAGER of a drugstore in Mansfield, Ohio, wrote us the following letter in 1975.

"Back in 1955, what started out as a weather gag ended up as one of the strangest and most unexplainable things that we ever had happen. The kid brother of one of the high school boys working for me came into the store with a baby snapping turtle about one and a half inches across. I felt sorry for the tiny turtle and proceeded to make a deal with the boy. For two comic books and a chocolate soda, the young snapper was mine. Just for a gag, the boy's brother and I dragged out an old aquarium, put sand and gravel on the bottom, and added three large stones — one at each end plus one in the middle. We marked the aquarium in three equal parts with 'Fair,' 'Changeable,' and 'Rainstorm.'

"Then we put in about three inches of water and the turtle, set the aquarium on one of our display shelves facing the soda fountain counter, and proceeded to solemnly tell people that where the turtle was at 6 P.M. would tell what the weather would be the next day.

"This first day was June 23, and a nicer day was never under way in this part of Ohio. The barometer was steady, and radio and TV forecasters, as well as the newspapers, were all telling what fine weather was in store for the weekend. It was going to be great for picnics, golf, sailing, and so on. The only sour note of the day came at 6 P.M., when the turtle was perched on top of the far-end rock of the section marked 'Rainstorm.' Grudgingly, we chalked up his first forecast — rainstorm — and everybody, including us, laughed like hell.

"Came 3 A.M., and there came up a sudden combination goose-drownder and gully-washer rain, along with high winds, hail, and lots of noise, taking down a few trees plus a few roofs in the area.

"To make a long story short, the turtle hit it right every day for fourteen days before making his first miss on July 7. We kept the record for a hundred days. Shortly after we stopped, he went into hibernation, and eventually he passed on to wherever good turtles go after leaving these worldly shores. Out of the one hundred days, he missed only fifteen times. We used to get phone calls every evening from people wanting to know where the turtle was that night — and sometimes we had as many as forty people in the store at six o'clock to see for themselves.

"The only part of a theory I have, and it doesn't make sense, is that the tank sat straight north and south, and the north end was the stormy one. Why? I don't know and can't even guess." ✻

Making a Cloud in a Bottle

PLACE ONE-QUARTER cup of water in a clean bottle that is fairly big in diameter and has a small mouth. Set the bottle on a table and shine a flashlight through it in such a way that the beam of light is at right angles to the viewer. Apply pressure to the bottle by blowing into it as if trying to blow up a balloon. Release the pressure and see what happens. A very few cloud droplets may be visible, reflecting from the beam of light. Now light a match and hold it near the opening of the bottle. Blow out the match. It is not necessary to get any of the visible smoke into the bottle.

Repeat the process of pressurizing the air and releasing the pressure. With enough change in pressure, a white cloud should appear, filling the bottle with thousands of tiny cloud droplets, each reflecting the light. If you apply pressure again, the cloud will disappear; releasing the pressure will bring it back as before.

This experiment never fails (well, hardly ever) to cause even the most nonscientific person to gasp at what a little dirt (the combustion particles from the match) will do.

Courtesy of Mark Urbaetis.

———————

Possibly it's easier than it looks here.

Old-Fashioned Cures for the Common Cold

Plenty of rest always accompanies a good cold remedy — and sometimes that's the hardest part.

Kids are always getting colds during the winter. And modern science has yet to figure out a cure. So the Almanac recently asked readers to send in their favorite cures from their childhood days. Here are the three we liked best.

FIRST PRIZE

FATHER AND BROTHER ran trap lines during the winter months. Being a thrifty man by nature, Father used as much of anything that came to hand as he could.

Skunks were quite prevalent in those days, so naturally we had a good supply of skunk furs stretched on boards in the basement.

Father boiled the carcasses to feed the chickens and, after scraping the pelts, rendered the fat.

This grease had several uses around the farm. It could be used to oil harnesses, boots, or a squeaking axle in a pinch. Another use I remember quite well. Whenever one of us caught a cold, Mother's remedy was to sprinkle sugar on onion pieces and feed us a spoonful at bedtime. Father's remedy was to slather skunk grease on our chests. All the time I was in grade school, I seldom had a cold. I might catch one — but after that, nobody came close enough the rest of the winter to give me another.

— *Lura O'Briant, Oxford, Iowa*

SECOND PRIZE

At age fourteen, I came home from school with a nasty cold. Later that evening, while I sat with fever, watery eyes, and runny nose, huddled in a blanket doing my homework, my elderly Great-aunt Mary said she had an old remedy for my cold. I groaned at the thought of an "old remedy," perhaps in the form of cooked tree bark or worse.

Finally, with homework done, I headed for bed. Aunt Mary stopped me with steaming cup in hand. "Drink this, and you will feel much better." Marveling at the excellent health of my tall, slender, seventy-five-year-old aunt, I emptied the cup, asking, "What did I drink?" With a warm smile and never-you-mind look, she tucked me into bed.

Waking after a night's peaceful sleep, I asked her for the recipe. She said, "I cooked a chopped onion in water, discarded the onion, and added milk and a pinch of black pepper."

This became my favorite cure for the common cold. To this day, some forty years later, I think of Great-aunt Mary when the sniffles and chills begin — and start chopping the onion.

— *Ann McGraw, Defiance, Ohio*

THIRD PRIZE

The only way to cure a cold is to catch it before it gets you down. At the first hint of a cold or the flu, sip the following tea. (Mix a batch ahead, using 2 handfuls of mint and 1 handful of each of the other ingredients.)

Mix the leaves of spearmint, red raspberry, catnip, mullein, and comfrey with red clover flowers and rose hips. Steep about 2 tablespoons of the mixture in hot water with a sprig of white pine bark (don't omit this key ingredient — the white inner bark is best) for about 10 minutes. Put the white pine bark sprig in your cup and pour in the tea. Sweeten with honey if desired. Drink about 3 cups a day, adding another sprig of bark for each cup.

Get plenty of rest.

— *Kayo Fraser, Goldcreek, Montana* ✺

Hand an egg timer to children whose temperature must be taken. They can watch the passage of time and remove the thermometer themselves.

– 1979 –

If the World Were a Village of 1,000 People...

The following statistics (calculated for the year 1991) provide young people as well as old with some perspective on the current population of our earth.

By Donella H. Meadows

- If the world were a village of 1,000 people, it would include:

584 Asians
124 Africans
95 Eastern and Western Europeans
84 Latin Americans
55 Soviets (including Lithuanians, Latvians, Estonians, and other national groups)
52 North Americans
6 Australians and New Zealanders

- The people of the village would have considerable difficulty communicating:

165 people would speak Mandarin
86 English
83 Hindi/Urdu
64 Spanish
58 Russian
37 Arabic

That list accounts for the mother tongues of less than half the villagers. The other half would speak (in descending order of frequency) Bengali, Portuguese, Indonesian, Japanese, German, French, and 200 other languages.

- In this village of 1,000, there would be:

329 Christians (among them 187 Catholics, 84 Protestants, 31 Orthodox)
178 Moslems
167 "nonreligious"
132 Hindus
60 Buddhists
45 Atheists
3 Jews
86 other religions

- One-third (333) of the 1,000 people in the world village would be children, and only 60 would be over age 65. Half the children would be immunized against preventable infectious diseases such as measles and polio.

- Just under half of the married women in the village would have access to and use modern contraceptives.

- The first year, 28 babies would be born. That year, 10 people would die, 3 of them for lack of food, 1 from cancer; 2 of the deaths

40 percent of its cropland — that owned by the richest and best-fed 270 people. Excess fertilizer running off this land would cause pollution in lakes and wells. The remaining 60 percent of the land, with its 17 percent of the fertilizer, would produce 28 percent of the food grains and feed 73 percent of the people. The average grain yield on that land would be one-third the harvest achieved by the richer villagers.

THE VILLAGE would have buried beneath it enough explosive power in nuclear weapons to blow itself to smithereens many times over. These weapons would be under the control of just 100 of the people. The other 900 people would be watching them with deep anxiety, wondering whether they could learn to get along together; and if they did, whether they might set off the weapons anyway through inattention or technical bungling; and if they ever decided to dismantle the weapons, where in the world village they would dispose of the dangerous radioactive materials of which the weapons were made. ✹

would be of babies born within the year. One person of the 1,000 in the village would be infected with the HIV virus; that person most likely would not yet have developed a full-blown case of AIDS.

- With the 28 births and 10 deaths, the population of the village in the second year would be 1,018.
- In the original 1,000-person community, 200 people would receive 75 percent of the income; another 200 would receive only 2 percent of the income.
- Only 70 people of the 1,000 would own an automobile (although some of the 70 would own more than 1 automobile).
- Of the 670 adults in the village, half would be illiterate.
- The village would have 6 acres of land per person, 6,000 acres in all, of which:
  700 acres would be cropland
  1,400 acres pasture
  1,900 acres woodland
  2,000 acres desert, tundra, pavement, and other wasteland
The woodland would be declining rapidly; the wasteland would be increasing. Other land categories would be stable.
- The village would allocate 83 percent of its fertilizer to

CHAPTER 7

Facing Marriage, Family & Career

OVER THE PAST 203 YEARS, all the Almanac's editors seem to have been in agreement that young people facing marriage, family, and career made up the segment of readership most in need of advice. Even though it has always been apparent that this particular age group is least likely to take it. At any rate, in every edition young people have been lectured ad nauseam to work hard, pay off all debts, send their children to school, plan ahead, avoid procrastination, be cheerful, practice thrift, stay off the booze, and on and on. In the years following the Civil War, the advice took on a rather desperate tone as the editors pleaded with their young readers to stay on the farm, forget about those city lights, and, for God's sake, not be bamboozled into moving west. All to no avail, as we know. In this chapter, therefore, we concentrate on readers' contributions. Their advice probably had no more effect on the younger generation than the dreary harangues of the editors — but at least they're more fun. ✸

Young, in love, and with a new baby. Life is perfect (for the moment).

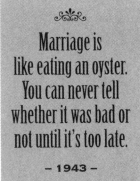

Secrets of a Successful Marriage

*Four Almanac readers — representing Colorado,
Virginia, Missouri, and Iowa — reveal their thoughts
concerning lifetime partnerships.*

WHAT'S LOVE GOT TO DO WITH IT?

MY PARENTS were Dutch farmers. In 1941, my first year teaching, two young men were calling on me. One was a neighbor, Albert, who was underfoot frequently; the other was a black-haired Irish lad I had met in college and who came around off and on for three years. When I returned home on my first free weekend after I started teaching, Irish met the bus, drove me home, and agreed to stay to Sunday dinner. He left shortly after dinner to go to work. My father looked over his glasses at me and said, "This young man, what do his folks do?"

"His father is a probate judge," I replied.

"He will never make a farmer?"

"Probably not," I admitted. No more said.

As I did the dishes with my mother, she asked, "Just how serious are you for this young man?"

"Oh," I replied, "I think he's cute. We get along pretty well."

My mother paused, then said, "You get along with Albert, too. But you don't want to marry a man you think you can live with. The one you marry is the one you can't live without!"

The black hair is silver now. We have six children. And he never did make a farmer. After World War II, he became a teacher.

— *Lura O'Briant, Oxford, Iowa*

SOMEONE TO WARM YOUR FEET ON

Recently, I approached my husband of thirty-five years. "What makes our marriage a success?" I asked.

"It's not a success," he answered, avoiding my eyes.

"Does this mean you're leaving?" I asked.

"Just as soon as I get through eating," was his reply.

Snatching for his slice of apple pie, my fingers did a sharp pivot in midair to scratch an imaginary itch on my nose as he warbled sweetly, "Honey, this has to be the best pie you've ever made!"

After washing the dishes, I passed him coming in from outdoors with a load of firewood under his arm. "You'd better be on your way," I threatened.

OPPOSITE: According to Almanac readers, less-than-successful marriages are those in which one side or the other insists on winning every argument.

"When I get through drying the dishes," he replied.

Later, as I saw him heading for the bedroom in his pajamas, all ready for the night, I said, "Still here?"

"Till tomorrow," he countered. "Gotta get you to church tomorrow and pick up the grandchildren for you to baby-sit tomorrow afternoon." Warming his always-cold feet on mine, he muttered something about my being the only one around with a checkbook.

Well, although he claims our marriage isn't a success, he's still around!

— *Marie Pemberton, Denver, Colorado*

WAKING UP A HALF HOUR EARLY

What is the secret of a successful marriage? Easy! It's a pot of coffee and thirty minutes of private time each day.

Twelve years ago, I married a wonderful woman with two sons. She began bringing two cups of coffee to bed each morning. We even set the alarm a half hour earlier than necessary so we would not have to rush through our eye opener. Our sons soon learned that we were not to be disturbed during our "private time" for anything less than a house fire. The activities of those thirty minutes varied. Sometimes we talked of trivial things, sometimes of money matters or future plans. Sexual activity filled that half hour on occasion. Other times we sat silently in the early

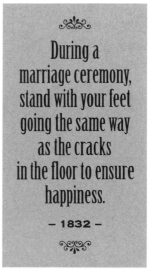

During a marriage ceremony, stand with your feet going the same way as the cracks in the floor to ensure happiness.

– 1832 –

morning darkness holding hands while drinking coffee with the other hand.

The boys are grown and on their own now, but my wife and I still have our "private time" in the morning. Sometimes I make and deliver the coffee; usually she does. We've decided to give the marriage another twelve years to see if it works out. I suspect that in the year 2000, we'll decide to try it for another twenty-four years, just to give the marriage a chance.

— *Ed Baldwin, Norfolk, Virginia*

DON'T WAIT AROUND FOR AFFECTION

My mother was an indifferent cook, but she made a marvelous holiday cookie. We tried without success to copy her efforts. When we asked how much of an ingredient she used, her reply was, "I don't measure. I just use as much as I need." Long practice had taught her how much that was.

In bringing up children, you need to love and guide them as much as needed. In marriage, instead of stewing about whether your partner is doing his share, think about what you need to do to make this enterprise a success. If you hold back, waiting for the other person to give you a certain measure of love, trust, and affection, he may do even less. If you respond with unmeasured love, you will get back in kind. At least this advice has worked for me for forty years of marriage. But I still can't make Mama's cookies successfully.

— *Patricia Paden, Stark City, Missouri* ✳

The Language & Sentiment of Flowers

Useful if the meanings are understood
by both parties . . .

FLOWER	MEANING	FLOWER	MEANING
Amaryllis	Beautiful but timid	Jonquil	Desire; affection returned
Anemone	Forsaken; illness	Larkspur, pink	Lightness; fickleness
Apple blossom	Preference	Lavender	Mistrust
Arborvitae	Unchanging friendship	Lilac, purple	First emotions of love
Arbutus	Thee only do I love	Lilac, white	Youth
Bachelor's button	Hope; single blessedness	Lily of the valley	Return of happiness
Barberry	Petulance; ill temper	Marigold	Grief; chagrin
Bittersweet, nightshade	Truth	Mayflower	Welcome
Bluebell	Constancy	Mint	Virtue
Burdock	Importunity; touch me not	Milkweed	Hope in misery
Buttercup	Riches	Mistletoe	I surmount everything
Cardinal flower	Distinction; preferment	Morning glory	Coquetry; affection
Carnation	Pure and deep love	Mountain ash	I watch over you
Chrysanthemum	A heart left to desolation	Narcissus	Egotism; self-love
Clover, 4-leaf	Be mine	Nasturtium	Patriotism; splendor
Clover, white	I promise	Oleander	Beware
Columbine, red	Anxious and trembling	Pansy, purple	You occupy my thoughts
Coreopsis	Always cheerful	Peach blossom	I am your captive
Crocus	Cheerfulness	Peony	Ostentation; anger
Daffodil	Unrequited love	Phlox	Our hearts are united
Dahlia	Dignity and elegance	Poppy, white	Sleep; oblivion
Daisy, field	I will think of it	Primrose	Modest worth; silent love
Daisy, garden	I share your feelings	Rhododendron	Agitation
Dandelion	Oracle; coquetry	Rose, red	I love you
Fern	Sincerity	Rose, white	Silence
Forget-me-not	Do not forget	Rose, wild	Simplicity
Foxglove	Insincerity	Rose, yellow	Infidelity
Fuchsia	Taste; frugality	Rosemary	Remembrance
Geranium	Silliness	Sage	Domestic virtue
Gladiolus	Ready armed	Scotch thistle	Retaliation
Goldenrod	Encouragement	Snapdragon	Presumption
Hawthorn	Hope	Sweet pea	A meeting
Heliotrope	I adore you	Sweet William	Gallantry; finesse; dexterity
Hibiscus	Delicate beauty	Tuberose	Dangerous pleasure
Holly	Am I forgotten?	Tulip, red	Declaration of love
Honeysuckle	Devoted love	Violet, blue	Faithfulness
Hydrangea	Vainglory; heartlessness	Violet, white	Purity; candor; modesty
Iris	A message for thee	Yarrow	Cure for the heartache
Ivy	Friendship; marriage	Zinnia	I mourn your absence

*When it came
to put-downs, nobody
did it better than
"The Honeymooners."*

Language & Sentiment of Insults (& Squelches)

Like flowers, useful for those special occasions . . .

INSULTS

- He's the type who approaches every subject with an open mouth.
- She says that whenever she's down in the dumps, she gets a new hat. Obviously, that's where she gets them.
- He makes you wish birth control could be made retroactive.
- He heard that hard work never killed anybody, but he's taking no chances on being its first victim.
- He believes he's still as good at attracting women as he never was.
- He didn't mind her enjoying crackers in bed until he came home and discovered a crumb in the closet.
- They were married for better or worse. He couldn't have done better, and she couldn't have done worse.
- He goes through life pushing doors marked "pull."
- It's useless to ask him to act like a human being. He doesn't do imitations.
- He's so dull he can't even entertain a doubt.
- He's thinking of quitting drinking — he's beginning to see the handwriting on the floor.

SQUELCHES

- Next time you pass my house, I'll appreciate it.
- Why don't you get yourself x-rayed to see what people see in you?
- Don't ever change — I want to forget you exactly as you are.
- I've got two minutes to kill, so tell me all you know.
- You have a striking face. How many times were you struck there?
- Why don't you leave and let live?

*From Louis A. Safian, 2000 Insults for All Occasions.
©1965 by Louis A. Safian.*

> **A man will break his fist on a locked door, but a woman will look for the key.**
>
> — 1914 —

The Difference Between Men & Women

Before going too far in life, it's best to know . . .

ONE WAY in which men are different from women is that men are smarter. They have been running the world since it began, and it has gotten better and better every year, until finally it turned out like it is now.

Another difference is that men have stronger muscles than women. This, of course, has nothing to do with why they have been running the world. It would be dangerous to suggest it.

Most of the world's inventive geniuses have been men. Men have brought us wars, cereal boxes that can't be opened, the national debt, politics, violence, television, plastics, and the idea that men are smarter than women. They've created this big stuff by themselves.

Women, on the other hand, have brought us only men.

For a long time, human society has been organized along the lines of a chicken yard: the males do the crowing, and the females do the work. Here and there the roosters are beginning to notice, though, that there are more and more chicken yards without roosters, but there are no chicken yards with only roosters. It makes them nervous. Recently, the hens have begun to stand up for themselves, a rising problem.

— Bandera Brandt, Poteet, Texas

It all started when Adam and Eve noticed that men and women were created a little differently. . . .

A Sharp Knife & Some Stout Thread

That was all the father-to-be had, or needed, to perform the first cesarean delivery in America on a cold Virginia night in 1794. It's a tale of incredible courage — and love.

By C. Brian Kelly

ONLY TWENTY-FIVE, married barely a year, red-haired Pennsylvanian Jessee Bennett faced the most momentous decision of his young life, with two other lives — those of his wife and their unborn child — entirely dependent on his skill and courage.

The scene was a log cabin in rural Edom, Virginia; the time was the wintry night of January 14, 1794; and the problem was obstructed delivery of Elizabeth Hog Bennett's baby. Hours after Elizabeth had gone into her difficult labor, it appeared that either mother or child must die.

Repeated attempts at a forceps delivery, with Dr. Alexander Humphreys of nearby Staunton consulting, had failed. The next step normally would be a craniotomy — forced removal of the infant from the birth passage by crushing its head and simply pulling it out, a fatal procedure.

The courageous mother, sure she would die, begged the two men to save her baby by any means possible. Jessee Bennett proposed a cesarean delivery, which had never before been attempted in North America.

Oh, no, absolutely not, vowed the veteran practitioner Humphreys — he would have no truck with anything so risky. When Bennett became more insistent, Humphreys stomped out into the snowy night.

But Bennett was himself a physician, albeit somewhat untried, who had "read" his medicine in Philadelphia and completed his training at the University of Pennsylvania. Now, mind made up, he wasted no time. In minutes, Elizabeth was rendered unconscious by a large dose of laudanum. She was placed on a makeshift table of two planks set across barrels. Two black servant women helped by holding her, and the patient's sister, Mrs. William Hawkins, also assisted.

"With one quick sweep of the knife," as one historian was to say, the gambling doctor made his incision. Seconds later, he lifted forth the child — a girl. Then with the remark, "This shall be the last one," he quickly removed both of his wife's ovaries. By the flickering lamplight, he sewed up the wound with stout linen thread normally used to stitch heavy clothing.

Amazingly, both mother and child lived to a ripe old age. So did Bennett himself, serving as an army surgeon in the abortive Whiskey Rebellion; representing his later home of Mason County, now West Virginia, in the Virginia General Assembly; and figuring as a witness in the trial of Aaron Burr at Richmond.

Aside from saving his own wife and child, what Bennett had managed that January night was the first abdominal operation in America, the first cesarean section, and the first ovariectomy. But the nation's medical community would not learn of his feat for another century or so. For many years, the first cesarean section was credited to Dr. John Richmond, an Ohio physician, for an abdominal delivery performed thirty-three years after Bennett's.

News of the real pioneer delivery was finally reported in 1891 by Dr. A. L. Knight, a family friend, in a history of the Kanawha Valley of West Virginia. This obscure citation was fol- lowed by a report in the *West Virginia Medical Journal* nearly forty years later. Undoubtedly, Bennett himself could have sped things up, but he is said to have once explained, "No doctor with any feelings of delicacy would report an operation he had done on his own wife." ❁

How to Raise Perfect Children

Although modern psychology frowns on thinking of a child as a lump of bread dough, there are, in fact, certain analogies between baking a fine loaf of bread and raising a child to be proud of.

By Susan Peery

BOTH BREAD BAKING and child rearing can be performed successfully without any prior experience. And although there are dozens of books of written recipes for both, the savvy baker and the wise parent soon realize that books can only give clues, for in real baking and real life, you have to do a lot of reading between the lines. Here's a baker's half dozen guidelines you can adapt to suit your circumstances.

1. Set aside enough time. When baking bread, any attempt to hurry the rising and take shortcuts will result in an inferior product, crumbly and full of holes. Similarly, raising children takes time, and there's no way you can hurry through certain phases or skip any developmental stages, even if it's the stage where all the little darling does is say "No!" and "Why?" Something complex and tasty is happening to the yeast (and the child) at every stage, something that will contribute to the ultimate flavor and texture. How long does this take? It takes as long as it takes, time beyond Zen.

2. Use fresh ingredients for every batch. Dedicated bakers often develop a sourdough starter that they use for successive bakings of bread, but the ingredients they add to the starter must be fresh, of the highest quality, and suitable for the desired result. Parents who decide to embark on more than one effort at child rearing might use the same "starter" to give a certain harmony to the family, but they will soon discover that the second child may have very different needs from the first, and ingredients will have to be varied accordingly. You may have one child whose temperament is that of sourdough rye, followed by another who most resembles a popover. Don't try to stir all that heavy rye flour into your popover; adjust your recipe to fit. And don't forget to add a little sugar to feed the yeast, for, as Mary Poppins says, "A spoonful of sugar makes the medicine go down."

3. Provide a warm environment for the dough. Yeast breads are sensitive to temperature: too cold, and the yeast won't activate; too hot, and the yeast will die. The temperature range that's right has plenty of latitude — it's the extremes that cause failure. Children also need warmth, and plenty of it, lest they fail to thrive, but not so much that they smother. And without that basic, life-giving warmth, all the educational toys, great books, and natural-fiber baby clothes in the world won't make a whit of difference.

4. Knead with a light but firm touch. The baker must knead thoroughly, turn the dough often, pat it gently, get to know its character, and handle it with attention and consistency. (This is why homemade bread is infinitely better than commercial bread mixed in large vats and kneaded with giant dough hooks, untouched by human hands.) On a bread-baking day, the baker knows that there's a lot of time for other activities between risings, just as long as he or she keeps one eye on the dough. Children, too, will thrive with the right mixture of independence and hands-on attention, and they need safe boundaries just as the baker needs a bowl to mix the dough and control the rising.

5. Prepare for the unexpected. The only way to do this is to be flexible enough to abandon preconceived notions about results. Have all the ingredients on hand for poppy seed bread — except poppy seeds? Substitute: try sesame seeds, or raisins and grated orange rind, or a handful of chopped herbs. Always dreamed of coaching your son's Little League team — except he wants to spend the summer practicing his clarinet? Adapt: take him into the city to hear some good jazz. Maybe your daughter will like baseball.

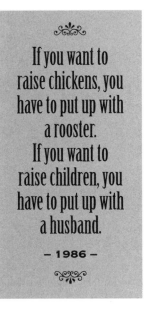

If you want to raise chickens, you have to put up with a rooster. If you want to raise children, you have to put up with a husband.

— 1986 —

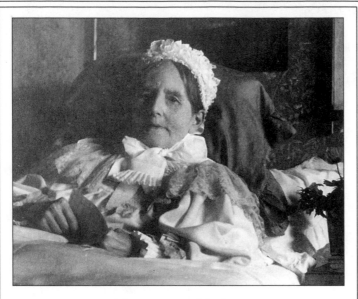

Advice from Mother

Maybe sometimes, just sometimes, that advice is not all you'd like it to be.

THIS HAPPENED during the last two weeks of my mother's life, after she was diagnosed as terminally ill. My parents' home was filled with their two daughters, three sons, and two sons-in-law, who gathered at her side. Like a mother hen tending to her chicks, my mother rose to the occasion, proving to us that cancer had not taken control of her quick wit and ability to be in charge.

On one of these long-remembered evenings, my sister and I washed and dressed Mom for bed in the only thing comfortable to her — Daddy's well-worn flannel pajamas. As the three of us sat on the edge of the bed, we asked her if there was anything else she needed. Mom shook her head. Then slowly raising her heavy-lidded eyes, she turned to me and motioned me to come closer. With a heavy heart, knowing these would be some of the last words my mother would say, I leaned down toward her small figure. Her words came, faint but clear.

"Maureen," she whispered, "always keep your hair permed!"
— *Maureen Kelleher Taylor, West Tremont, Maine*

6. Don't get in over your head. Don't promise to bake twenty loaves in one weekend if you have a small oven. As a parent, don't get stuck making rules you can't enforce. For instance, you can't really *make* children go to sleep — it's good enough to tell them that they must go to bed (hey, you can make it fun — cuddle up and read a story or two); they don't have to go to sleep. (Reverse psychology is especially effective with five-year-old contrarians, who will fall asleep in thirty seconds — right after you tell them they can stay awake if they want to.)

7. Presentation matters. Every good cook knows that you can dress up the plainest meal to make it seem special. Place your homemade bread on a nice bread-board and surround it with artfully arranged slices of cheese and cold meats. Use pretty napkins and good dishes. Then sit back and watch the food disappear. The child-rearing corollary is this: **Always buy the right lunch box.** Fussy eaters *can* be dazzled by the right container, by sandwiches cut into star shapes with cookie cutters. Little hurts *can* be fixed with Kermit the Frog bandages. Reluctant readers *can* be lured into literacy gradually with judiciously chosen comic books. It's just the art of friendly persuasion, of getting your bread and your kids raised. ✹

Predicting How Many Children You'll Have

It worked for this reader . . .

FIRST, TAKE AN ORDINARY wooden pencil with an eraser and stick a threaded needle into the center of the eraser. Then lay your left arm on a table, with the palm of your hand facing up. Pick up the thread and dangle the pencil above your wrist. The pencil will begin to move. If it moves across your wrist, you'll have a boy. If it moves up and down your arm, you'll have a girl. The pencil will go in circles between each signal for more than one child, although twins will be treated as one. It will come to a stop or wiggle when the count is finished. (*Note:* This works for men or women but not for women using birth control pills.)

For those who doubt the veracity of this method, let me cite my own case. Several years ago, I had my tubes tied after I was divorced. At the time, I had two teenage sons, and the pencil would always stop after signaling two boys.

Then I married again and, for fun, tried the method on my new husband, who had no children. The pencil swung up and down his arm and then across his wrist — a girl and boy still to come! As for me, the pencil signaled two boys, a girl, and then another boy.

Well, I had my tubes untied and am now the mother of Eric, 18; Ben, 16; Collette, 3½; and Jack, 20 months.

Courtesy of Karen C. Okey, Erie, Pennsylvania.

35 Ways to Get Rich Without Doing Any Work!

Some of these folk beliefs about money go back thousands of years. Or you might hear some of them on the street tomorrow . . .

By Tim Clark

THE FAMOUS MILLIONAIRE John D. Rockefeller is said to have had three simple rules for anyone who wished to become rich: (1) Go to work early. (2) Stay at work late. (3) Find oil.

It worked for Mr. Rockefeller, but a lot of people would prefer an easier way to wealth. That's why folklore is full of curious notions about money: who is born to be rich; how to marry a rich man; how to attract money by eating certain foods or wearing special clothes. The following folk beliefs are part of the rich collection of folklore at Harvard's Widener Library. The state or ethnic group in which each belief was recorded is listed in parentheses.

ARE YOU BORN TO BE RICH?

- Give a newborn baby a penny. If she clutches it tightly, she will be rich. (Kansas)
- If your thumbs turn up at the ends, you will be a spendthrift. (Indiana)
- If your fingerprints make circular lines, you will be able to save lots of money. (Indiana)
- If a baby's initials spell a word, he or she will become wealthy. (North Carolina)

GET WEALTHY WHILE YOU SLEEP

- If you dream of apples, you'll do well in business. (Indiana)
- Dream of emeralds, and you'll inherit money. (Indiana)
- A dream with gold in it indicates good commercial prospects. (Indiana)
- Dreaming about oysters is a sign of prosperity. (Indiana)
- If you dream about a tooth being filled, you will recover lost valuables. (Indiana)
- Dream of snakes, and money will arrive the next day. (Nebraska)
- Red coals in your dreams are a sign you'll become rich. (Alabama)
- If a nest filled with eggs appears in your dreams, you will die rich. (North Carolina)

THE EASY-MONEY DIET

- Swallow a raw chicken heart to bring money. (Indiana)
- If you can swallow the bubbles on your coffee without breaking them, you will earn a fortune. (Maine)
- The blood of a blacksnake, swallowed warm with whiskey, will give you the power to earn more money than anyone else. (Nebraska)
- Eat hog jowls and black-eyed peas on New Year's Day for a prosperous year. (Alabama)
- When making a pie, trim the crust all around without changing hands. It's sure to bring riches. (New England)

PETS OF THE RICH AND FAMOUS

- If a buzzard lands on your house on a Monday, you'll receive money soon. (African-American)
- A three-colored cat attracts money. (Maine)
- If a bluebird flies into your house, it brings wealth with it. (Georgia)

HOW TO MARRY MONEY

- A bride should always have an old coin, preferably one handed down from her mother, in her shoe at the

Money does,
on occasion, grow on trees.

wedding. It ensures prosperity. (Georgia)

- If you dream of your future husband bringing you water in a cup made of gold or silver, you will marry a rich man. (New England)
- If your shoes are worn-out on the sides, you will marry a rich man. (New England)
- Marry in September's shrine, all your days are rich and fine. (Alabama)
- A girl with hairy arms and legs will marry a rich man. (Alabama)
- If you see a goldfinch on a holiday, you'll marry a millionaire. (Alabama)
- A big wife and a big barn

will never do a man any harm. (Pennsylvania Dutch)

DRESS FOR SUCCESS

- A piece of money tied to or around your ankle prevents poverty. (African-American)
- If a man walks around with his hat brim turned up behind, he's got money to spend. (New England)
- If a man has one pant leg tucked in his boot and one pant leg out, he has money. (New England)

AVOID THESE COMMON MISTAKES

- After a tooth is pulled, don't put your tongue in the empty space. A gold tooth

will grow there. (Indiana)
- If you look at a naked woman, you will lose all your money. (African-American)
- Never sweep your floors on New Year's Day; you'll sweep away all your money. (Alabama)

CRUDE BUT FOOLPROOF

- Spit on the first money you receive each day. (North Carolina)
- When you see a white horse, put your little finger under your lips and spit over it to attract money. (Maine) ✺

Scrooge had a hard-driving, competitive personality. The Ghost of Christmas Yet to Come should deduct five years for that.

How Long Will You Live?

THE AVERAGE LIFE EXPECTANCY for men and women in the United States is at best a very general statistic. Individual life spans vary greatly; some of the reasons are genetic, but some are under a person's control. To get a more precise idea of how long you may expect to live — and what you can do about it — find the average life expectancy for someone your age in the accompanying chart, then answer the lifestyle questions below.

YOUR AGE NOW	AVERAGE LIFE EXPECTANCY FOR MEN	FOR WOMEN
25	73	79
35	74	80
45	75	80
55	76	81
65	80	84

1 Enter your basic life expectancy from the table above. _____

2 For every 5 years that your father lived past 70, add 1 year to your average life expectancy. Add 1 year for every 5 years your mother lived past 78. _____

3 If you are single, deduct 1 year for each decade you are unmarried after age 25. _____

4 If you are married, add 5 years. If there is an unusual amount of strife in your family, subtract 2 years. _____

5 If you live in a city, subtract 2 years. If you live in a small town or on a farm, add 2 years. _____

6 If you have been either poor or wealthy most of your life, subtract 3 years. _____

7 If you're over 40, subtract a year for every 5 pounds you weigh above your best weight. Men only: Deduct 2 years per inch that your waist measurement exceeds your chest measurement. _____

8 If you exercise moderately but regularly, add 3 years. If you regularly do vigorous exercise, add 5 years. _____

9 If you have a hard-driving, competitive personality or are often tense, deduct 5 years. Add 5 years if you're usually cheerful and easygoing. _____

10 If you drink heavily, subtract 5 years; very heavily, 10 years. If you take recreational drugs, subtract 5 years. _____

11 If you smoke ½ to 1 pack of cigarettes daily, subtract 3 years. If you smoke 1 to 1½ packs, subtract 5 years; 2 packs, 10 years. _____

12 If you have regular medical and dental checkups, add 3 years. If you're often ill, subtract 2 years. _____

13 If your diet is high in fats, salt, and sweets, deduct 4 years. If you eat a balanced diet with plenty of fruits, vegetables, and low-fat proteins, add 4 years. _____

YOUR LIFE EXPECTANCY _____

From Practical Problem Solver, ©*1991, The Reader's Digest Association, Inc.*

> Take out
> a six-month loan
> in the fall, and
> the winter will fly by
> like nothing.
>
> **ABE WEATHERWISE**

CHAPTER 8 ⇥
Those Busy Middle Years

*A*s EVERYONE KNOWS, there's not much time for quiet reflection and philoso-phizing during those busy middle years. So the advice most valued during this period of our lives is the down-to-earth, practical variety. In other words, advice from which you can derive recognizable benefit relatively quickly. "Do not trust a man who keeps late night hours," the Almanac (in the 1930s) quoted a seventy-six-year-old woman from Ohio. "He is a poacher, a thief, a smuggler, a drunkard, a womanizer, a counterfeiter, or a vampire." Nothing vague about that. The same woman maintained that "the juice from pickled walnuts, taken a teaspoonful at a time, is a sovereign remedy for depression." For sure.

So it is with much of the advice chosen for this chapter. Castration, apparently, will prevent baldness. Don't eat four slices of pizza before attempting to set the world record for continuous forward somersaults. And if for some reason you want to shorten your life, go to balls in the thinnest possible dress, dance 'til in complete perspiration, and then go home through damp air. Good, practical advice for 1857 — and today. ✺

Down-to-earth advice is particularly useful during those high-wire middle years.

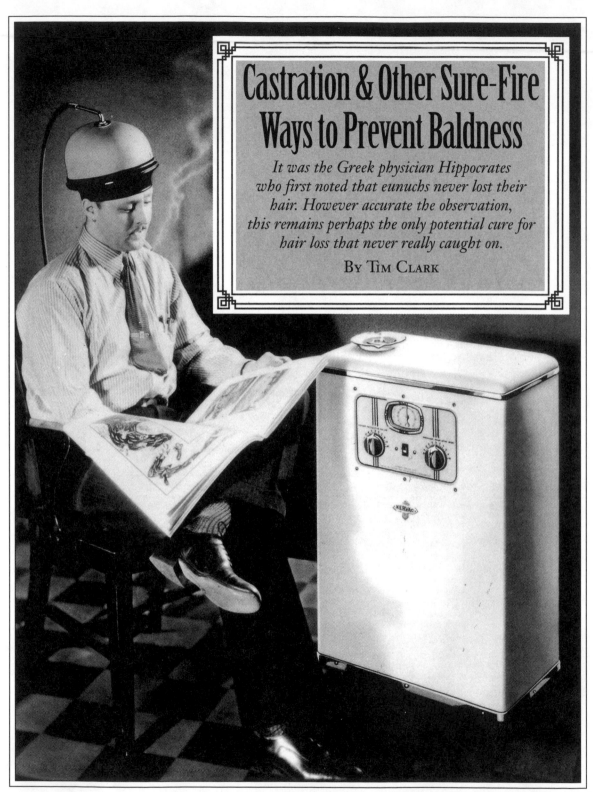

Castration & Other Sure-Fire Ways to Prevent Baldness

It was the Greek physician Hippocrates who first noted that eunuchs never lost their hair. However accurate the observation, this remains perhaps the only potential cure for hair loss that never really caught on.

By Tim Clark

BALDNESS IN MEN is not quite as inevitable as death and taxes. About one in every five men begins to go bald right after puberty and is completely bald by age thirty; three out of five gradually lose their hair between the ages of thirty and sixty. Only one out of five keeps a full head of hair after age sixty, and even then, his hair will literally grow thinner, each individual hair diminishing in diameter about 15 percent between ages fifty and seventy.

It's not a new problem, either. Mexican cave paintings show that prehistoric men lost their hair, too. The earliest recorded baldness remedy dates back to 4000 B.C., when the mother of King Chata of Egypt recommended rubbing the balding head vigorously with a mixture of ground-up dog's paws, dates, and asses' hooves, cooked in oil. In later centuries, desperate men massaged their scalps with everything from boiled snakes and cow urine to the blood of murdered babies, to no avail.

Such treatments were bound to make men grumpy. A biblical example is that of Elisha, who, when he was taunted by the children of Bethel shouting, "Go up, thou bald head," cursed them in the name of the Lord. What happened next should be a lesson to anyone who has ever uttered the phrase "chrome dome" — ". . . there came forth two she-bears out of the wood, and tare forty and two children of them."

Even fame was of little consolation, as we learn from a fifteenth-century chronicler who noted that "Julius Caesar was ballyd whereof he had displaisir." In fact, Caesar was said to have worn his hero's laurel wreath mostly to conceal his baldness. And Napoleon Bonaparte, who also went in for laurel wreaths, fretted enough about his receding hairline to discuss cures with Czar Alexander of Russia. All three probably would have agreed with Professor Harley Parker, Victorian England's "Eminent Hair Scientist," who remarked that losing one's hair "exercises on the mind a very depressing and disheartening influence, leading us, insensibly, to find fewer charms in society, less beauty in nature, and, in short, to view everything through a less hopeful medium."

The search for the causes of baldness has taken some bizarre turns. At various times and in various places, baldness has been blamed on using a dead person's comb, allowing rain to fall on a bare head during the dog days, and allowing cut hair to be thrown out where birds can make nests with it. The shape of the skull has been blamed, on the premise that a high-domed configuration tightens the skin so much that blood flow to the follicles is reduced.

OPPOSITE: Men have attempted to cure baldness with everything from boiled snakes and cow urine to machines like this.

Babies haven't any hair;
Old men's heads are just as bare;
Between the cradle and the grave
Lies a haircut and a shave.
— *Samuel Hoffenstein*

Touché or Something to Ponder

SOME YEARS AGO, an Iowa farmer was out plowing on a Sunday and urging on his mule with spiced-up phrases like, "Git on you — of a — old —ing —!" when a thin-nosed town lady rode past his field on the way to church. As she overheard his colorful monologue, she stopped and called out to him.

"Caleb! 'Tain't fittin' you actin' the way you do!" she said. " 'Tain't enough you workin' on the Sabbath 'stead of goin' t' church like respectable folk, but you got to curse out that poor dumb creature of the Lord with language that ain't fittin' for decent ears. Jest wait'll I git to town and tell everybody about you!"

The old farmer squinted at the town lady, spat on the good brown earth, and replied, "Maud, it's true I ain't much of a churchgoin' man, and it's true my talk don't speak like a parson. But I've a mind that in the Lord's eye it's a damned sight better to swear and mean no harm than to pray and mean no good." *Courtesy of Gordon V. Carr.*

A slightly different version of this theory came from two psychiatrists who speculated that laughter and broad smiles, by tightening the muscles controlling the scalp, could constrict the blood supply and make the jolly man bald.

Folk remedies have included eating parsnips daily; rubbing the scalp with an onion; regular bathing with salt water, sage tea, or rum; and pomades of buffalo oil, axle grease, cow manure, and mud from a riverbed that has been dry at least two months. Another prescription is to spread milk or cream on the bald spot and let a cat lick it off.

The Greek physician Hippocrates tried a number of remedies, including a poultice of cumin, crushed horseradish, beetroot, and pigeon droppings. More significantly, he observed that boys castrated before puberty to become eunuchs never grew bald. It was a sure-fire cure, but one that never gained much popularity.

But Hippocrates was on to something: a link between male sex hormones and baldness that is still being unraveled by scientists today. Aristotle thought that sexual intercourse caused baldness; Rabelais, to no one's surprise, thought the opposite. For a while, bald men could take comfort or even pride in the theory that hair loss was caused by an unusual abundance of the male sex hormone testosterone. However, more recent research shows that bald men actually have no more of the hormone than men with hair. They do have twice the number of testosterone receptors and double the amount of an enzyme needed for testosterone metabolism — thus, they have an increased capacity to bind the hormone, which causes the death of hair follicles. "You're really not more virile," said researcher Marty Sawaya.

Scientists also know there is a genetic connection, but the latest findings show that it is not as simple as was once supposed. For a while, it was thought that a male child could look at his maternal grandfather and see his own fate. But scientists now say that baldness can be passed down from either parent and that brothers may not be affected in the same way.

So the quest for a cure continues, and in the meantime, bald men buy toupees, or have new hair woven to the old, or get their scalps tightened or dotted with plugs of hair from other parts of their bodies. A few even cover up small bald spots with spray paint.

Then there are those few — call them a fringe element — who continue to grin and bare it. They belong to the Bald-Headed Men of America, an organization founded in 1974 by John T. Capps III of Morehead City, North Carolina.

"There are two kinds of bald-headed men," Capps says. "The kind who can't believe it or accept it — that's the group that has made remedies popular since Caesar — and the kind who like it and wouldn't have it any other way." Capps counts himself among the latter and has a simple explanation for his minority status. "The Good Lord created only a few perfect heads — the rest He had to cover with hair!" ✪

> To cease and desist
> indulgence in
> the nicotine habit,
> boil two cigar butts
> in a pint of water
> for an hour,
> adding water to
> replace that lost.
> Let cool and drink.
>
> – 1934 –

A happy gathering of some of the Bald Headed Men of America, founded in 1974.

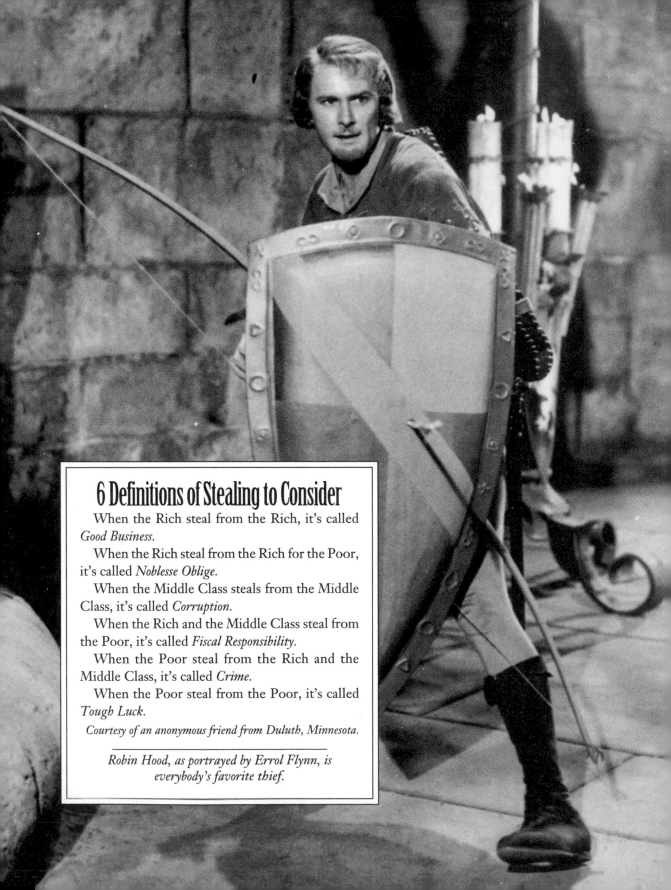

6 Definitions of Stealing to Consider

When the Rich steal from the Rich, it's called *Good Business*.

When the Rich steal from the Rich for the Poor, it's called *Noblesse Oblige*.

When the Middle Class steals from the Middle Class, it's called *Corruption*.

When the Rich and the Middle Class steal from the Poor, it's called *Fiscal Responsibility*.

When the Poor steal from the Rich and the Middle Class, it's called *Crime*.

When the Poor steal from the Poor, it's called *Tough Luck*.

Courtesy of an anonymous friend from Duluth, Minnesota.

Robin Hood, as portrayed by Errol Flynn, is everybody's favorite thief.

How to Be a Failure as a Town Official

After all, you wouldn't want to have to do it forever.

MANY OFFICIAL positions in a small town are filled by individuals who have been pressured into those jobs by others. If you are a reluctant town office holder, here are fifteen basic steps that, if adhered to carefully, should relieve you of any further civic responsibilities:

1. Neglect your public relations image.
2. Take public office when you know you don't have the time and energy to perform the expected duties.
3. Ignore your fellow officers. Act as a committee of one.
4. Use the position to promote your own self-interest or personal gain.
5. Accept gifts or favors from individuals or firms.
6. Try to fit into someone else's moccasins.
7. Make promises to individuals and groups that you cannot deliver.
8. Be an expert on all things and to everybody.
9. Be content to just "hold office." "Let George do it."
10. Let honest differences degenerate into personality conflicts.
11. Stay in your own back yard and town office. Don't visit other successful communities that have "lucked out."
12. Keep the public uninformed.
13. Hold closed meetings. What they don't know won't hurt them.
14. Listen to the loudest. Be misled by the most "noise" or the most letters from special-interest demands.
15. Be a yes man. Don't express your honest convictions if they are in the minority. Polarize your group. Generate heat instead of light.

W. C. Fields as town sheriff: how not to succeed in office.

Anyone can try to set a world record for push-ups (below). But besides Ashrita Furman, how many have even thought about setting a record for underwater pogo-stick jumps (opposite)?

Practical Advice on Becoming a World Record Holder

As we approach middle age, it becomes apparent to most of us that, alas, we're probably not going to become famous and go down in history. But wait! There are still ways! And they're not all that difficult . . .

By Suki Casanave

OST PEOPLE think Ashrita Furman is nuts. In fact, this guy just might be one of the nuttiest people on earth. Still, his name does keep showing up in *The Guinness Book of Records.* There he is in the 1993 edition under pogo-sticking, joggling, somersaults, hopscotch, and milk bottle balancing. All told, over the last dozen or so years, he's set more than thirty official records, including some that were still standing in 1993. Nutty or not, Ashrita Furman apparently knows a thing or two about this business of achievement.

The question is, How does he do it? What does it take? Let's face it. We've all spent our share of time contemplating the possibility of becoming famous for something. But by now you may have given up your dream of dodging deftly past the defense for the winning touchdown. You've abandoned the possibility of warbling your way to success as a country music star. And you never really looked that good in a tutu. What else is there?

Ashrita Furman, record holder among record holders, just might have the answer: it may be that you simply haven't found the right outlet for your talents — or, more accurately, maybe you haven't found the right talents. Take the *Guinness Book*, for example. This collection of world records and unusual human feats is one route to fame — or a few lines of it, at least. It's second only to the Bible in number of copies sold, it's updated every year, and unlike the Bible, anyone can get in. Even you.

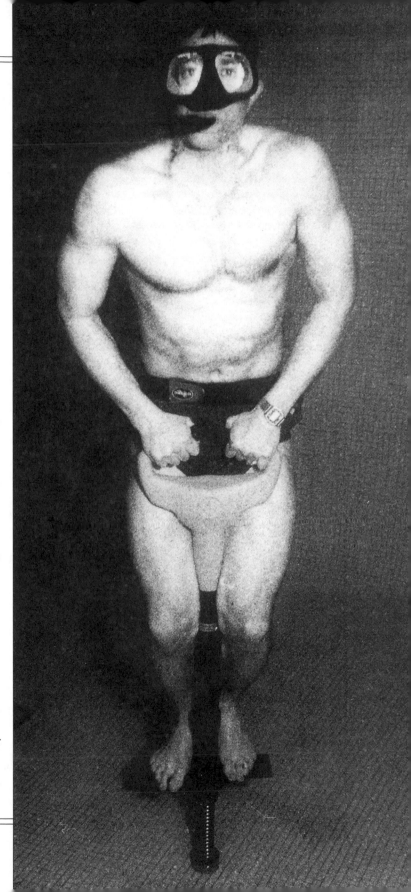

Ashrita, a 5-foot 10-inch, 165-pound health food store manager from Queens, New York, insists there's nothing special about him. "Anybody has the capability," he says. In fact, he loves it when people break his records. "It just inspires me to do better." Well, there it is: an invitation to break the records of the world-record-holding champion himself. He even offers some tips for success based on his past experience. Study them carefully. He knows what he's talking about.

MOTIVATION IS IMPORTANT

First of all, you need the right initiation experience. For Ashrita, a self-described former wimp once destined for life as a lawyer, it all started with a bike race. For twenty-four hours, Ashrita rode, along with thousands of others, around and around Central Park. Unlike most of the others, he pedaled 405 miles, coming in third overall — a remarkable feat, especially given the fact that he'd hardly trained at all. "I wasn't in great shape physically," Ashrita says, "so obviously it had to be something much deeper."

Ashrita credits his success to a combination of meditation and sheer determination. As part of his study of Eastern philosophy with teacher Sri Chinmoy, Ashrita, whose given name is Keith, received his new name, which means "protected by God" — not a bad appellation given the grueling stunts he has undertaken. Although he admits that some of his feats draw more laughter than awe, each one, he says, is a challenge. The bike race was only the beginning.

FIND THE RIGHT ACTIVITY

One time early in his career of breaking records, Ashrita managed to juggle 100,000 times in a row, drawing an admiring crowd as he stood in Grand Central Station. Pleased with his creativity, he submitted his record to the *Guinness Book*, only to find that they wouldn't accept it because the category didn't exist. Since then, he's set some unusually creative records, but he advises new record breakers to stick to established categories.

KNOW THE RULES

The second time Ashrita tried to get into the book, he went after the pogo-sticking record for the most continuous jumps. He completed 100,000 jumps in a record thirteen hours, and then, as if that weren't enough, he continued. He actually jumped for twenty-four hours, only to find that the occasional rests he took after each hour were longer than the legal time allowed. The record was void. Not an encouraging start.

CHOOSE THINGS YOU LOVE

Ashrita's all-time favorite record is one he set in Japan, where he pogo-sticked up and down the foothills of Mount Fuji for eleven and a half miles. "It was exhilarating, and the Japanese people loved it," Ashrita says. "Of course, someone eventually broke my record on flat land — they did twelve miles. But I broke it right back again and did thirteen." In contrast, the record for continuous clapping just wasn't worth defending. "I did it for fifty hours — one hundred forty claps a minute audible at one hundred yards," Ashrita says. "Eventually, somebody broke my record, but it was just too boring to do again."

DON'T FORGET MEDIA COVERAGE

This is an important part of the verification process. (You also must have official witnesses who are not friends.) "They can't send fact checkers all over the world," Ashrita notes, "so they expect you to provide some proof." But it can be hard to attract press attention. The key is to surprise them. If you're going for the deep-knee-bend record, for example, don't just do it in a gym. "It's kind of hard to get anybody to come watch a guy stand and squat for hours on end," says Ashrita, who figured what he needed was a piano. He rented a baby grand, got a friend to play, and then stood on top and huffed his way to another record.

You may not, of course, always want media coverage. When Ashrita was trying to set a somersaulting record, for example, *People* magazine was there to cover the story, along with several local newspaper reporters and TV crews. Ashrita was so nauseated after the first two miles that he thought

Don't eat four slices of pizza before attempting to somersault for twelve miles.

Tried & True Advice for Shortening Your Life

(1857)

1. Wear thin shoes on damp nights in rainy weather.
2. Go to balls in the thinnest possible dress, dance 'til in complete perspiration, and then go home through damp air.
3. Surfeit on hot and very highly stimulating dinners.
4. Beginning in childhood on tea, go, one step to another, through coffee, chewing tobacco, and drinking.
5. Marry in haste.
6. Keep children quiet by teaching them to suck candy.
7. Eat without time to masticate food.
8. Follow an unhealthy occupation because money can be made by it.
9. Contrive to keep a continual worry about something or nothing.
10. Retire at midnight and rise at noon.
11. Give way often to fits of anger.
12. Neglect to take proper care when a simple disease first appears.

Another tried and true tip: Leap before you look.

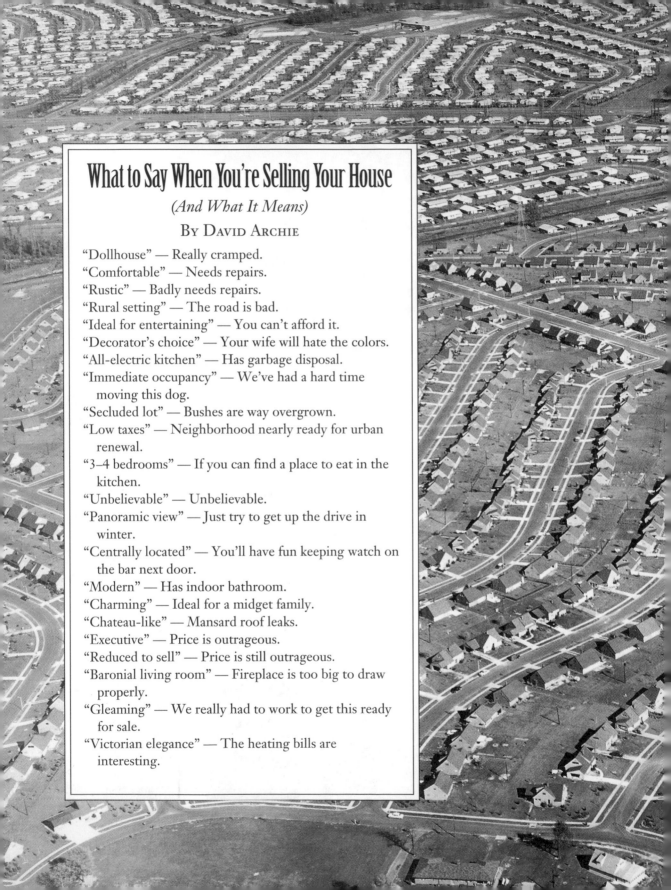

What to Say When You're Selling Your House

(And What It Means)

By David Archie

"Dollhouse" — Really cramped.

"Comfortable" — Needs repairs.

"Rustic" — Badly needs repairs.

"Rural setting" — The road is bad.

"Ideal for entertaining" — You can't afford it.

"Decorator's choice" — Your wife will hate the colors.

"All-electric kitchen" — Has garbage disposal.

"Immediate occupancy" — We've had a hard time moving this dog.

"Secluded lot" — Bushes are way overgrown.

"Low taxes" — Neighborhood nearly ready for urban renewal.

"3–4 bedrooms" — If you can find a place to eat in the kitchen.

"Unbelievable" — Unbelievable.

"Panoramic view" — Just try to get up the drive in winter.

"Centrally located" — You'll have fun keeping watch on the bar next door.

"Modern" — Has indoor bathroom.

"Charming" — Ideal for a midget family.

"Chateau-like" — Mansard roof leaks.

"Executive" — Price is outrageous.

"Reduced to sell" — Price is still outrageous.

"Baronial living room" — Fireplace is too big to draw properly.

"Gleaming" — We really had to work to get this ready for sale.

"Victorian elegance" — The heating bills are interesting.

he'd have to quit. Another tip: Don't eat four slices of pizza before attempting to somersault for twelve miles.

MORAL SUPPORT CAN'T HURT

Just because you can't have friends as official witnesses doesn't mean they can't come along and cheer you on. Sometimes they may even be able to save your life. Ashrita once decided to trace the entire route (more than twelve miles) of Paul Revere's midnight ride between Charlestown (in

RULES TO LIVE BY

10 Rules of Behavior

(According to Thomas Jefferson)

1. Never put off till tomorrow what you can do today.
2. Never trouble another for what you can do yourself.
3. Never spend your money before you have it.
4. Never buy what you do not want because it is cheap; it will be dear to you.
5. Pride costs us more than hunger, thirst, and cold.
6. We never repent of having eaten too little.
7. Nothing is troublesome that we do willingly.
8. How much pain have cost us the evils which have never happened.
9. Take things always by the smooth handle.
10. When angry, count ten before you speak; if very angry, a hundred.

Jefferson had a rule for every occasion.

Boston) and Lexington. In the opposite direction. By somersaulting. (That's 8,341 somersaults.) Throughout the feat, friends walked alongside to keep him from getting run over by traffic.

Occasionally, a police escort may be more appropriate — if you decide, for example, to row along the New Jersey Turnpike from New York City to Philadelphia. Ashrita's rowing feat began on the Staten Island Bridge as a policeman sang, "Row, row, row your boat" over the loudspeaker on his car. Seven hours later, sailing along on his rowing machine with wheels, he arrived in the city of Philadelphia, having been escorted by the police force in every town along the way.

CHOOSE APPROPRIATE WORKOUT CONDITIONS

Although Ashrita is not on any sort of rigid training schedule, there are times when he must put aside all pride in pursuit of his goal — well, almost all pride. "People already think I'm crazy," he points out. "What do you think they'd say if they saw me out there somersaulting around a track?" The master tumbler trains for his somersaulting records in the dark of night on a two-hundred-meter dirt track at his old high school. He wears a helmet and a strip of foam to protect his backbone, but he comes home covered with mud and grit.

When Ashrita decided to try to pogo-stick to the top of the Canadian National Railway's tower in Toronto, the logical place to train was the five flights of stairs in his father's office building. "People would pass me as I sweated and hopped my way up those stairs. Usually they were too afraid to say anything," Ashrita says. Occasionally, they'd attempt a polite question: "Ah, is that good exercise?"

ALWAYS HAVE ANOTHER GOAL

"The great thing about this," says Ashrita of his record-breaking career, "is that it's one adventure after another. There's no limit to what we can do. I found another record I'm really excited about — running a marathon wearing a forty-pound pack on my back and combat boots." Sound like fun? Perhaps something with a bit of cultural flair would appeal more. Six years after his grueling twelve-mile somersaulting stunt, Ashrita says he's ready for the Great Wall of China. He's also considering deep knee bends in quicksand.

See, there are plenty of things to choose from. All you need are a few records that get you really excited, revved up, and ready to roll — or run or juggle or row or jump — and off you go. Grab your pogo stick and start practicing. ❂

> Advice to newly elected politicians: "Until you know what's going on, vote no."
>
> — VREST ORTON —

RULES TO LIVE BY

6 Rules for a Long Life

(According to Satchel Paige)

1. Avoid fried meats, which angry up the blood.
2. If your stomach disputes you, lie down and pacify it with cool thoughts.
3. Keep the juices flowing by jangling around gently as you move.
4. Go very light on the vices, such as carrying on in society. The social ramble ain't restful.
5. Avoid running at all times.
6. Don't look back. Something might be gaining on you.

Courtesy of Ira Truckine, Tampa, Florida.

Satchel Paige, pitcher and philosopher.

Why It's Not Advisable to Name a Cow After Your Neighbor's Wife

It can turn into an incredible misunderstanding.

By Lael J. Littke

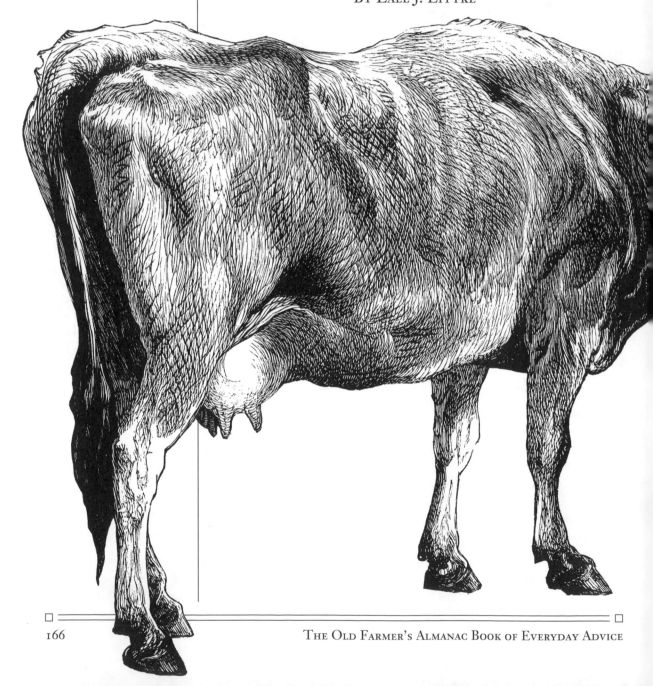

ALL THE TROUBLE started, Ivy Turner speculated later, because her husband, Sylvester, liked to name his cows after the men from whom he bought them. Hence, in his sizable herd, along with the Muleys and Bossys and Rosies he had raised himself, he had a Bill Higgins, a Walt Adams, an Asa Bell, and a Harvey Thompson. No one in town minded Sylvester's calling his cows by these names, least of all the men concerned. As a matter of fact, the men considered it kind of a mark of distinction, and they all had a good time about it when they gathered at the Owl Billiard Parlor in nearby Burnsville each Saturday night.

Things would have gone along peaceful and happy if Sylvester hadn't bought two cows from Thaddeus Cooley. Since he couldn't name two cows Thaddeus Cooley, he up and named the second cow after Thaddeus's wife, Viola. Right from the first, Viola didn't take much to the idea, but she didn't say much of anything about it until Sylvester started noising it around that Viola Cooley was going to have a calf.

Ivy was out hoeing in her lettuce garden one morning when Clyde, the mailman, beckoned her over to where his car was stopped by her mailbox.

"Hear tell Viola Cooley's fit to be tied," Clyde told her.

"Oh?" Ivy said. "What's the matter with Viola?"

Clyde cleared his throat. "Don't especially like Sylvester's naming a cow after her. Says it ain't fittin'."

Ivy nodded. "Well, it isn't. I told Vest it would stir up a ruckus, but nothing would do but that he name that cow 'Viola.' I'll tell him he's got to change it. Though 'Viola' does seem to fit that cow so well. Her pretty eyes remind me of Viola Cooley's somehow. Well, I'll just tell Vest he's got to call her 'Beauty' or something."

Clyde sent Ivy's words along the line as he went on his rounds, only by the time it got back to Viola, after being filtered through Blanche Neiderhauser and Millie Higgins and Nell Olsen and Althea Thompson, the only thing that remotely resembled Ivy's original words was that Viola had eyes like a cow.

"Look like a cow, do I?" shrilled Viola to Millie Higgins, further altering Ivy's intent. "Well, I always did think Ivy Turner had it in for me. I'll just bet it was her that put Sylvester up to naming that cow after me. It

> Hired people are more likely to be praised into good conduct than scolded out of bad. Always commend them when they do right. To cherish the desire of pleasing in them, you must show them that you are pleased. This applies equally well to children.
>
> – 1855 –

If 3 Rules Are Enough

(1800)

Keep your feet warm,
your back straight,
and your head cool.

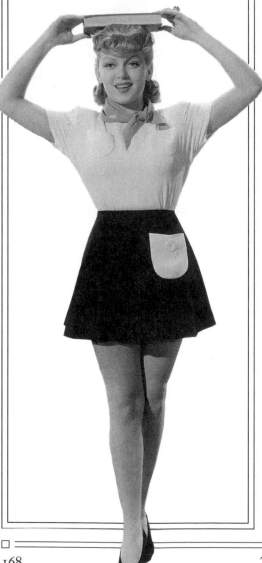

was her, that's who it was. She hasn't been friendly at all since I got my new maroon overstuffed set. She's jealous, that's what she is. Jealous. Naming a cow after me."

Viola's speech was duly transmitted to Ivy, whose first thought it was to run over to Viola's and get the matter straightened out before any more rumors started turning the air blue. But the truth of the matter was that she *was* a little jealous of Viola's new maroon overstuffed set, especially since Viola, in a spirit of generosity with only just a tinge of pride, had offered Ivy her old brown set, thus implying that even her old castoffs were superior to what Ivy had. So after she thought about it, Ivy decided she wouldn't be caught dead going over to Viola Cooley's.

There were those ladies in town who were on Ivy's side. After all, Viola *had* been a little uppity since she got that new furniture.

Viola got so mad at Ivy that she took to walking backward out to feed her chickens, since if she walked normally, she would be facing Ivy's house and might catch a glimpse of Ivy out hanging clothes or working in her garden. One day she tripped over a milk bucket Thaddeus had left on the path and broke her leg. Nothing would do but that she blame it on Ivy.

The county newspaper compounded the problem by printing a short article on page 5 stating that Viola Cooley, a cow owned by Sylvester Turner, had kicked over a milk pail and broken her leg. It further stated that the cow would probably have to be shot. Such errors were to be expected in the weekly *Grouse Valley Tribune*, since it was a well-known fact that Art Haskins, publisher, editor, reporter, and printer, kept a bottle hidden under the press that did not contain printer's ink.

Naturally, Viola Cooley took it hard, being laid up with her broken leg and all.

"I can't abide a woman who would stoop so low," she wept to Millie Higgins, blaming the article on Ivy, too. "You can just pass it along that I'm sitting here with my busted leg just waiting for her to come and apologize."

"Apologize!" Ivy was indignant when Clyde told her

the news. "In a pig's eye, I'll apologize. *If* I'd of done anything, I'd march these two feet right over there and apologize my head off."

And so the battle raged. The womenfolk hadn't had anything important to talk about since Soren Ernsrad's wife, Helga, ran off with the Italian linoleum salesman, so they made the most of it.

No one knows how Viola ever got Thaddeus to take a hand in the fight. It was unheard of for a man to interfere in a hen fight, but interfere he did. At least he went over to speak to Sylvester about it one evening.

"The wife's all het up about it," Thaddeus told Sylvester, hanging over the bars of the fence while Sylvester replaced a broken post. "Do you reckon as how you could call that cow by some other handle? Maybe Rosie or something?"

"I already got me a Rosie," said Sylvester.

"Well, Bossy then. It's not me that objects to it, Vest. Why, I kind of take a personal interest in that cow named Thaddeus Cooley. But womenfolk, they're different."

Sylvester tamped the dirt around the new post and leaned on his shovel. "I'd sure like to oblige you, Thaddeus, but look at it this way. That poor little heifer is due to have her first calf just any day now. She's got used to being called Viola.

The Best Rule: "Keep It Simple"

FRANCIS W. DAHL

"Thaddeus, I never did right understand women," Sylvester said, "but I do understand cows. Now, if I was to switch names on Viola right now, she'd go plumb off her feed and no telling what would happen to her when her time comes. I'd sure hate to upset her right now."

"Course not," said Thaddeus. "She's likely to be a good milker, and it would be downright crazy to do anything to put her off her feed. I'll just tell Viola to forget about the whole thing."

Having done his duty, Thaddeus bade Sylvester good-bye, tipped his battered hat to Ivy, and strolled across the field toward his home.

Ivy had pretended not to hear any of the conversation, but after Thaddeus left, she discovered that she had hoed off an entire row of young lettuce plants.

When Viola, the cow, finally produced her calf, as pretty a little creature as you ever laid eyes on, Art Haskins, still befuddled about the whole situation, put a short filler at the end of a column reporting that Viola Cooley had given birth to a calf and was doing fine in spite of her broken leg.

It wasn't long until Viola the cow began attracting attention in a new way. For such a small cow, she gave enormous quantities of milk that consistently tested remarkably high in butterfat content. The owner of the local creamery allowed as how he'd never seen a cow test so high.

With Sylvester's consent, he inserted an article in a state agricultural newsletter and contacted the state agricultural college. Sure enough, Viola was a champion, and pretty soon interested parties from all over the state came to see the pretty gentle little Jersey and offer Sylvester large sums of money for her.

It was a big day in Grouse Valley when the Cherry Milk Company from upstate sent a representative down to talk to Sylvester about using Viola for their mascot. Her picture would appear on every can of Cherry Milk and her name would be used in all the company commercials, to say nothing of personal appearances on TV and maybe an occasional tour of state and county fairs. She would be allowed to live at the Turner farm, since the slogan of the Cherry Milk Company was "Cherry Milk comes from cheery cows," and they didn't want to take a chance of making Viola unhappy by moving her to unfamiliar pastures.

"We'll retain her name," said Mr. Trumbull of the Cherry Milk

Omigosh! or Always Read the Fine Print

A CHICAGO WOMAN attending the movies one day had a very bad headache and, groping in her purse, over a period of two hours took what she assumed to be five aspirin tablets, with no relief. When she left the theater, she discovered to her horror that she had taken concentrated food tablets for plants. Reading the label in fear and trembling to see if she had been poisoned, she found it all reassuring until she came to a footnote that read, "Each tablet is equivalent to 1 shovelful of manure."

Courtesy of Grace Smith Beers.

Company to Sylvester and Ivy and most of the people of the town who had assembled for the big event. "It's a good name for a cow."

Sylvester nodded, and Ivy was about to give assent, too, when she happened to glance over toward the Cooley farm. There stood Viola, leaning against the corner of her house. She looked lonely and forlorn as she watched the gathering at the Turner place. And all the trouble was because menfolk thought more of cows than they did of women.

"No," Ivy said all of a sudden. "No, you'll have to change her name. It's just too much to do that to her."

"I don't understand," stammered Mr. Trumbull.

"There's a limit," insisted Ivy. "Call the cow Elsie."

"But another company has Elsie," said Mr. Trumbull.

"Well, Bertha then. But not Viola. It's bad enough to call her Viola around here, but to advertise it all over the world . . . NO!"

"Now, Ivy . . ." Sylvester began.

"Don't 'now Ivy' me. You've had your little joke all these months, and look what it has done to poor Viola."

Mr. Trumbull glanced at the cow who stood cheerfully chewing her cud, a perfect advertisement for the Cherry Milk Company. "She looks fine to me," he said.

"I'd best explain," said Sylvester.

"You'd best do just that," Ivy said, "while I go over to the Cooleys'."

Viola was still standing by the corner of the house when Ivy arrived. She opened her mouth to speak as Ivy approached.

"I heard about how the milk company wants to use that cow for a mascot," said Viola softly.

Ivy hung her head. "I figured you had."

"They name roses after people," Viola continued softly, "but this would be the first time that there'd be a famous cow named after an actual person. I'd be right proud."

Ivy stared at her friend in stunned silence.

"Just imagine, my name being used on TV and everything," Viola said. "And can't you just see what Art Haskins will do to it in his paper? 'Viola Cooley, champion butter maker of the state and wife of Thaddeus Cooley, was chosen by the Cherry Milk Company to have a picture of her broken leg appear on all their cans of milk.' "

As Ivy and Viola remember it now, even though they lost that last news item, that's just about word for word the way it came off Art Haskins's little press. ❀

Two sparrows on the same ear of corn are not long friends.

– 1881 –

Ode to a Cow

SEVERAL READERS wrote the Almanac after the following was published in the 1936 edition to say it was the best advice they'd ever read anywhere.

When life seems one too many for you,
Go and look at a cow.
When the future's black and the out-
    look blue,
Go and look at a cow.
For she does nothing but eat her food,
And sleep in the meadows entirely
    nood,
Refusing to fret or worry or brood
Because she doesn't know how.

Whenever you're feeling bothered and
    sore,
Go and look at a cow.
When everything else is a fearful bore,
Go and look at a cow.
Observe her gentle and placid air,
Her nonchalance and savoir faire,
Her absolute freedom from every care,
Her imperturbable brow.

So when you're at the end of your wits,
Go and look at a cow.
Or when your nerves are frayed to bits,
And wrinkles furrow your brow;
She'll merely moo in her gentle way,
Switching her rudder as if to say:
"Bother tomorrow! Let's live today!
Take the advice of a cow."

CHAPTER 9

Retirement & the Golden Times

RETIREMENT wasn't a problem in the early days of the Almanac. You just found yourself sitting on the porch more and more while your children and grandchildren did the work on the farm more and more. It was a gradual thing. During this century, however, retirement for both men and women has become one of life's major milestones. You worry that suddenly you and your spouse will be sitting in your living room at ten o'clock on a workday morning — staring at each other.

Which brings us to the selections in this chapter. They're designed to help prevent that situation. You can enter a cow-chip-throwing or worm-fiddling contest, for instance. You might consider becoming a fishing guru. You might even consider an exciting new career, such as selling chicken feet to the Chinese. At this stage of your life, the point is to be happy. But remember this warning from the 1801 edition: "If we were content to be happy, that would not be difficult; but we are ambitious to be more happy than others, and this is difficult because others appear to be happier than they really are."

Some couples appear happier than they really are.

New Career Opportunities

As the writer discovered in 1988,
sometimes one can make good money selling things
other people would throw away. For example . . .

BY ART SORDILLO

GREASE

*I*N THE *Wall Street Journal*, you will always be able to find a cash-price commodity quote on grease (choice, white). Rendering fat and grease is a billion-dollar-a-year industry in the United States (grease is used in livestock feed), but before you can render it, you have to collect it. Tom Driscoll is the route manager for Baker Commodities in Vernon, California. Tom makes sure his drivers get out and get the grease. "We use a vacuum tank truck. It has a hose to suck it up." Tom sends his drivers out to fast-food establishments, taco stands, butcher shops — anywhere the oil boils and the suet sits. He wouldn't get really specific and talk numbers, but each truck (he has several) collects twenty-four thousand pounds of grease every other day, and according to Tom, "We've been in business quite a while."

FEATHERS

"Down is down right now," says Dorothy Hobbs with some disappointment. Dorothy and her husband, Don, know where to buy and sell feathers. They own Hobbs Feather Company in West Liberty, Iowa. At first Dorothy was hesitant to talk much about the company: "We have to be careful with our competitors." But in a business that's not just for the birds, the stakes are high. "We sell over one hundred thousand pounds of feathers a year: turkey, goose, duck, and fancy ones, too." The feathers are washed, dried, and fluffed right on the premises. Mostly, they're sold to fly-tiers and bedding companies. (The Hobbses also dye feathers in sixty-three different colors.) Dorothy is always looking to buy bird feathers and bird skins, so give her a call if you have any. Maybe you'll catch her on a good day, when the market for down is up.

CHICKEN FEET

An average chicken foot weighs an ounce. Rockingham Poultry Marketing Cooperative in Broadway, Virginia, has a lot of chicken feet. "We sell about fifty metric tons a month overseas, mostly to China," says Henry

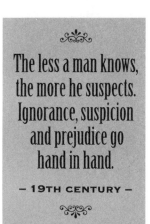

Fred Astaire and Leslie Caron (with ice cream), Daddy Longlegs.

Don't Mess with a 52-Year-Old Woman Carrying a Sundae

IT HAPPENED two days before Christmas 1986 in Albany, New York. A fifty-two-year-old woman had just purchased a large hot-fudge sundae (with both jimmies and nuts) at an Albany ice-cream parlor and was walking across a parking lot toward her car, carrying the sundae in a large plastic dish. Suddenly, a man confronted her and demanded her purse.

"She struck him repeatedly with the hot-fudge sundae she was carrying," said Sergeant Robert Wolfgang, a police spokesman, when interviewed by a UPI reporter later. "I know that sounds strange, but that's what happened."

Although the woman suffered a small cut on her hand, she was not seriously injured in what evidently was a rather short, one-sided struggle. The man fled, empty-handed, as soon as he could do so, but, as the woman described him to police officers, he was "a real mess."

Holler, vice president of sales. He continues, "They eat them spiced, as hors d'oeuvres." Holler gets serious when he discusses how the trade evolved. "In the chicken-foot business, it's important to sell a good product. Now most of your high-speed pluckers break the feet, so we came up with a better way — to see to it nobody buys a broken leg." Holler has succeeded where others have failed. He has cracked the overseas market. He doesn't like throwing around dollar figures but allows, "Let's just say that the new machinery we developed will pay for itself."

PIG TAILS

There's at least one part of the pig that doesn't go in a hot dog, and William Redd sells it: the tail. At Gwaltney Meat Packing in Smithfield, Virginia, Redd is vice president of sales and seems to have reinvented the squeal.

"Well, on average, I'd guess there's about three pig tails to the pound; 'course that depends on the size of the pig." Right. Pig tails go for about 45 cents a pound overseas. Redd sells most of his tails to South America, where they are pickled. We took his word for this. The next question was how many tails are sold. "Hard to say," he answered, "but we process about a thousand pigs an hour." ✸

Don't Bother Reading Any Instructions But These

GRASP THE GIZMO in your left hand. With your right hand, insert the doohickey into the little whosit just below the bright red thingamajig and gently — gently! — turn it in a clockwise direction until you hear a click. Attach the long thingamabob to the whatchamacallit. Do not under any circumstances allow the metal whatsit on the end to come in contact with the black plastic thingummy. Failure to follow these instructions will result in damage to the doodad.

Charlie Chaplin shows how it's done (Modern Times).

Weird Competitions You Can Enter

Don't know what to do with yourself these days? Well . . .

By Jamie Kageleiry

THE INTERNATIONAL WORM FIDDLING CONTEST

CARYVILLE, FLORIDA • LABOR DAY WEEKEND

Worms, last time we checked, didn't have arms. So fiddling must be sort of difficult. Unless, of course, one competes in fiddling *for* worms. And that's what this is. You plant a wooden stake in the ground and rub a metal bar (or a two-by-four or an ax head — you can be creative) across it to cause a vibration that magically calls the worms from the earth. The siren song is called "snoring" or "grunting." Whoever brings up the most worms wins a trophy.

"Sometimes the worms can be contrary," says former Caryville town clerk Ethel Lawrence. "The secret of success is rhythm." People have been coming to Caryville, on the shores of the Choctawhatchee River, every Labor Day weekend since 1976 for catfish bait. After the half-day competition, there's a huge fish fry or barbecue.

For more information, call the Caryville Town Hall: (904) 548-5571.

THE COON DOG DAY BARKING CONTEST

SALUDA, NORTH CAROLINA • FIRST SATURDAY AFTER THE FOURTH OF JULY

Anyone with a hound dog can enter the coon dog barking contest. The critter doesn't even have to be a purebred, "as long as it's not a cocker spaniel," Orbin Southern told us. Orbin is the president of the Blue Ridge Coon Club, whence come the judges for this annual event.

After a coon dog parade through Saluda (population 650) and a town dinner, the barking is on. Dogs are judged on beauty and barking. To win in the barking category, a hound must bark, bay, or howl more than any other dog in thirty seconds. A sublime barker can get in more than sixty barks in that time!

The contest has been held every year for more than forty years. Everybody and his or her hound are welcome, and Orbin will be glad to supply information: (704) 749-9554.

WORLD CHAMPIONSHIP COW CHIP THROWING CONTEST

BEAVER, OKLAHOMA (COW CHIP CAPITAL OF THE WORLD)
SATURDAY NEAREST APRIL 22 — OKLAHOMA DAY

"Cow chips" are exactly what you suspect they are. And people in Oklahoma's Panhandle really do throw them. As a matter of fact, one Leland Searcy, native Oklahoman, tossed a cow chip 182 feet 3 inches in 1979 for a world record that still stands.

> I'm over seventy years old and got all my natural teeth but one. The secret is to eat a dollop of raw veal bone marrow every day.
>
> – 1930 –
> MRS. A. KELLER

OPPOSITE: *Out on the plains years ago, cow or buffalo chips were used for fuel. This evolved into the cow chip throwing contests of today.*

Mark Twain's Tom Sawyer *is, of course, the inspiration for the National Fence Painting Contest in Hannibal, Missouri.*

This is no arbitrary competition — cow chips are historically significant. This part of Oklahoma is arid and fairly treeless. Years ago, local pioneers used to stock up on cow chips to use as fuel during the winter. Out they'd go with a wagon, and it became a sport, of sorts, to see from how far back one could throw a cow chip and have it land in the wagon.

These days you win, in any of four categories, by throwing your cow chip the farthest. As with the discus throw, some degree of accuracy is necessary, since boundaries define the throwing field. If a chip breaks up in flight, the portion flying the farthest determines the measurement. Chips must be Beaver County chips provided by the town.

Anyone is free to enter, and, says town scatologist Kirk Fisher, there's even a special category for politicians and people from the media, "since they're always throwing the bull anyway."

Call the Beaver Chamber of Commerce for information: (405) 625-4726.

NATIONAL FENCE PAINTING CONTEST

HANNIBAL, MISSOURI • FOURTH OF JULY

This contest is right out of Mark Twain, and it's held during Hannibal's National Tom Sawyer Days. Entrants should be between ten and fourteen years old and are encouraged to dress like Tom Sawyer by showing up with the following:

1. cutoff jeans
2. patch on right rear pocket
3. patch on knee
4. suspenders
5. straw hat
6. light-colored shirt, sleeves rolled up
7. bare feet
8. handkerchief in pocket
9. freckles
10. weed in mouth

Each contestant gets a brush and a bucket of whitewash, and the winner is the one who most quickly and accurately paints the fence. Looking the most like Tom Sawyer doesn't hurt. Here's the catch: unlike Tom Sawyer, contestants are not allowed to enlist help with the painting.

For more information, call the Hannibal Chamber of Commerce: (314) 221-1101. ✸

Don't Ask a Vermont Farmer More Than One Question

THE LATE VERMONT HUMORIST Al Foley loved to tell the following bit of country humor:

"A city guy stopped to watch a Vermont farmer clearing his field of stones. The city guy asked the farmer where all the stones came from. The farmer, after a long pause, said, 'The glacier brung 'em.'

" 'Where has the glacier gone?' the city guy asked.

"The farmer replied: 'Gone back for more stones, prob'ly.' "

A wall wide enough for a wagon.

The 4 Fundamentals of Successful Fishing

Retirement allows you time to do things carefully and right. Which provides pleasure in activities you might once have considered dull. Take fishing, for instance . . .

BY HAROLD F. BLAISDELL

1. BE IN THE RIGHT PLACE AT THE RIGHT TIME

ASSESS THE POTENTIAL of your immediate vicinity by prospecting. For more distant waters, write to the appropriate state or province fish and game department. General rules regarding the right time are as follows:

Trout: When water temperatures are between 50°F and 55°F. Fish metabolism (and feeding) reaches its peak when water temperatures are rising from the forties and entering the optimum range. For the fly fisherman, it's when mayflies are hatching and trout are feeding at the surface. The earliest hatches of the season usually occur in the middle of the day, but in summer they are mainly dusk-to-dark affairs. For the bait fisherman, the right time is early spring, and later on, when stream levels rise from summer showers. In lakes, fish with bait at the mouths of brooks whenever they are roiled by sudden storms and are sweeping dislodged food items into the lake.

Smallmouth bass: During the spawning season (late May and early June) wherever the law allows. (Cast to the shoreline with fly-rod lures: popping bugs or streamer flies.)

Largemouth bass: All-season feeders, with the correct depth of more importance than the timing. However, largemouths often cruise the shoreline after dark and will smash at surface lures that kick up a commotion. (Use a flashlight or lantern only sparingly.)

Northern pike and pickerel: All-season biters.

Walleyes: During spawning runs (late April and early May) where legal. After spawning (late May and well into June) along the shoreline, where they tend to cruise in schools.

2. FISH AT THE PROPER DEPTH

Determining the right depth is of critical importance, especially in lake fishing. Northern pike and pickerel, largemouth bass, and pan fish tolerate warm water containing relatively little oxygen. Consequently, they can be

For a weakness in the sight, take two ounces of the leaves of rosemary and put them into a pint of brandy. After three days, strain and filter through paper, make warm, and wash the inside of the eye every night.

– 1773 –
(QUOTED IN 1966)

413-

Just Don't Inhale

Advice for the ages . . .

ADLAI STEVENSON is reported to have given some sound advice to a man who was about to receive an honorary degree, the citation for which would be replete with inflated praise of his accomplishments. Said Stevenson, "Such exaggerated flattery should do you no harm, and perhaps will be of some benefit to you, provided you do not inhale."

caught throughout the season in the shallow water that borders weed beds, around sunken brush, and in the shade of overhanging trees. (Cast to the edge of the cover in which they lurk, or anchor so that bait can be lowered close to this edge.)

During warm weather, trout, walleyes, and smallmouth bass seek the cooler water and higher oxygen content of the thermocline. This is a relatively thin layer of water that, in lakes of substantial depth, separates the warm surface layer from the cold and somewhat stagnant layer at the bottom. The depth at which the thermocline forms varies from lake to lake, but it usually lies between twenty and thirty-five feet beneath the surface. Fish are not evenly distributed throughout the thermocline. Instead, they are attracted to those places where the lake bottom lies within this comfort zone. Such hot spots exist where sunken reefs rise into the thermocline and where the lake bottom drops away sharply to enter it. Electronic depth finders are of great help in finding such reefs and drop-offs, but they also can be located by trial-and-error sounding. Once you've found them, fish natural baits within inches of the bottom. Should you elect to troll, use sufficient weight to hold the lure close to the bottom.

3. USE THE CORRECT BAIT OR LURE

All natural baits and artificial

lures will take a wide variety of species of fish, but most species have particular preferences. The following list matches species with the baits and lures to which they respond most readily.

Trout: Best baits include night crawlers, small earthworms, virtually all insect larvae that can be hung on a hook, very small crayfish, and small minnows. Appropriate lures include dry flies, wet flies, streamers, and small to tiny spoons, wobblers, and spinners.

Largemouth bass: Big minnows and large crayfish are top baits. Effective lures consist of plugs, both surface and underwater, popping bugs, large streamers, bucktail jigs, "spinner baits," metal spoons, and specially rigged plastic worms.

Smallmouth bass: Medium minnows, crayfish, night crawlers, small frogs, hellgrammites, grasshoppers, and crickets are best. Among strike-winning lures are medium popping bugs, streamers, and plastic worm rigs.

Walleyes: Use small to medium minnows and night crawlers. One or two night crawlers strung on a worm gang and trolled behind a

No. 4 spinner is an old standby. Trolled plugs and wobblers are also

Don't Underestimate What Your Friends Might Do

DURING THE WINTER of 1976, Tennessee state senator Fred Berry was close to being the senate's official fossil for a few minutes. Berry, sixty-three, offered a bill to name an official state fossil, an official mineral, an official stone, and an official gem. Since the bill was offered late in the legislative session, it was amended by voice vote to make Berry the state's official fossil. Berry withdrew the bill.

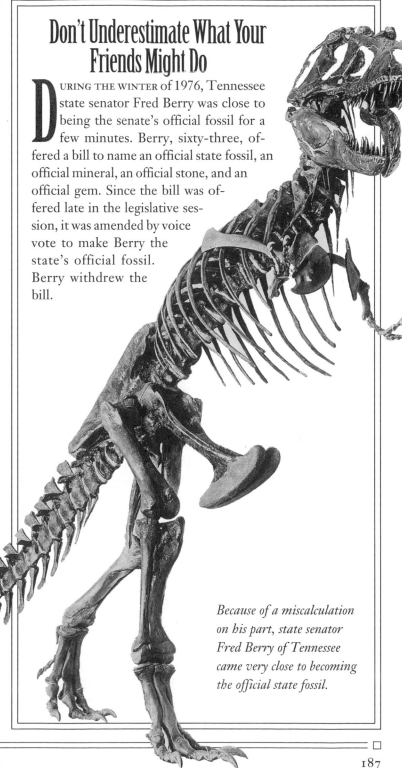

Because of a miscalculation on his part, state senator Fred Berry of Tennessee came very close to becoming the official state fossil.

effective. Walleye baits should be fished within inches of the bottom, and trolled baits and lures should be weighted to hold them just above bottom. Troll very slowly.

Northern pike and pickerel: Both feed almost exclusively on small fish, so minnows are the logical bait. Large, flashy spoons will produce savage strikes. In this category, the time-tested red-and-white Daredevil is without peer. For hair-raising strikes, tempt northerns with king-size popping bugs. Use a short wire leader or trace ahead of baits and lures, for both pike and pickerel will chop off fabric or monofilament lines with their sharp teeth.

4. USE THE PROPER PRESENTATION

You can be in the right place at the right time, fish at the correct depth, use appropriate baits and lures — and still return empty-handed because of faulty presentation. First, it is important to understand that the technique of winning bites or strikes splits into two completely different categories. Natural baits and their imitations appeal directly to fish hunger. Flashy, non-imitative lures excite fish to the point that they attack the lure.

Accordingly, natural baits and their imitations must be presented in a manner calculated to eliminate or disguise, to the greatest possible extent, all reasons for alarm or suspicion. To fool a critical trout, for example, a dry fly must respond freely to the whims of the current that bears it.

The problem, then, is that of minimizing the restraining influences of hook, sinker, and line. This is best accomplished by using the smallest hooks, the lightest sinkers, and lines and leaders of the finest diameter that can be used practically in a given situation. The inhibitive effect and anomalous appearance of big hooks, heavy sinkers, and coarse lines and leaders are grounds for immediate alarm and suspicion, and their use is perhaps the greatest single reason for lack of fishing success. Therefore, use every delicacy of presentation that circumstances will allow. If you obey this "commandment," increased catches are guaranteed!

Effective use of provocative, nonimitative lures is an altogether different matter. Here the secret of success is not finesse but erratic retrieves. Try a fast and steady retrieve, for example. Then, on the next cast, bring the lure back in short spurts. Let floating lures lie motionless for substantial periods, then apply the lightest possible twitches. Recast, and bring the same lure back to the boat so fast that it churns the water. Experiment constantly with the infinite variations that lie between these suggested ploys.

And if all else fails, be not bitter, but seek consolation in respect for your quarry. They meet fishermen on even terms, and only a poor loser begrudges a worthy opponent his share of victories. ✸

According to health agencies' records, people are in the most danger of receiving human bites on warm Saturday afternoons between 3 and 5 P.M.

– 1986 –

The Oldest, Wealthiest Dog in Florida

The thing was to keep him from sneezing . . .

WHEN ELEANOR RITCHEY, an oil company heiress, died in Florida in 1968, she left more than $4.2 million to the large menagerie of stray dogs she'd collected. The will further guaranteed a $17,000 care-taker's job. When the last dog died, the caretaker's job would ter-minate, and the remaining money would go to the College of Veterinary Medicine at Auburn University.

The last dog to die, in 1984, was a mutt estimated to be almost twenty years old. His name was Musketeer. His caretaker, anxious to keep his job, evidently went to some lengths to keep Musketeer alive as long as possi-ble. For instance, he hand-fed Musketeer vitamins, fresh hamburger, and spaghetti, a particular Musketeer favorite. He built Musketeer a $26,000 compound (using the inherited funds, of course). He also bought him an electronic bug zapper lest flies or fleas bother what was perhaps the world's wealthiest dog. And Musketeer hung on — and on. For the last several years, he hobbled rather than walked, barely opened his eyes for visitors, and usually fell over whenever he sneezed.

It was in the caretaker's interest to keep Musketeer alive at all costs.

47 Ways to Avoid Dying

All without giving up any of the stuff you really like to do . . . or eat.

By Tim Clark

Doctors and scientists are always telling us how to live longer. Usually their suggestions involve a healthier diet or lifestyle: eating less fat and more vegetables and fruits, getting more exercise, or giving up smoking. We wholeheartedly endorse these rigorous and unpleasant methods of extending life. But our research into centuries of American folk wisdom has turned up forty-seven *easy* ways of avoiding death by observing a few simple rules in everyday situations. These beliefs come from all over the country and were actually collected by students of folklore and anthropology. None of them was made up. Just remember: if you fail to observe these rules, we won't be responsible for the consequences.

HOUSEKEEPING HINTS

1. Don't take ashes out of the fireplace or stove between Christmas and New Year's Day.
2. Never place a broom on a bed.
3. Close umbrellas before bringing them into a house.
4. Avoid sweeping after sundown.
5. Never wash clothes on New Year's Day.
6. Don't, under any circumstances, shake out a tablecloth after dark.
7. Never wash a flag.
8. Keep cats off the piano keys.
9. Don't turn a chair on one leg.
10. Don't hang a dishcloth on a doorknob.
11. Never sweep under a sick person's bed; it will kill him or her.
12. Don't ever, ever rock an empty rocking chair.

RENOVATION & DECORATING

13. Never add on to the back of your house.
14. Don't cut a new window in an old house; the only way to avoid fatal consequences in doing this is to toss your apron through the new window, then jump through the opening yourself.
15. Never drive a nail after sunset.
16. Don't move into an unfinished house.
17. Avoid carrying axes, shovels, and other sharp-edged tools through a house. If you must take one inside, always take it out by the same door.
18. If you move out of a house, don't move back into it for a year.
19. Don't hang your sweetheart's picture upside down.
20. If a picture falls from the wall, don't pick it up.
21. Never carry a peacock's feather into a house.
22. Keep cut flowers out of bedrooms overnight.
23. Don't ever carry a bouquet of wildflowers indoors before May Day.

SEWING & FASHION

24. If you cut out a new dress on Friday, you must finish it that day.
25. Don't make new clothes between Christmas and New Year's Day.
26. Never hold a stick in your mouth while sewing.
27. Always sew cross-stitch on your underwear.
28. Don't walk around in one shoe.
29. If you see a will-o'-the-wisp while out walking at night, turn your coat inside out.
30. Never wear another's new clothes before he or she has worn them.
31. If you're a woman, don't make your own wedding dress. If you do, you will not live to wear it.

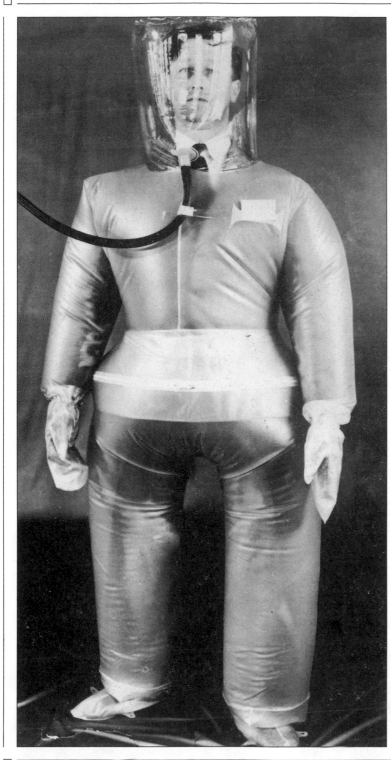

COOKING & TABLE MANNERS

32. Never set three lamps on a table at the same time.
33. Don't set the table backward.
34. Never serve thirteen at table.
35. Avoid drinking coffee at five o'clock.
36. Don't write on the back of a dish.
37. Never return borrowed salt.
38. Don't ever cross knives while setting the table.
39. Be sure that someone else cooks your birthday dinner.
40. Don't put two forks at one place setting.
41. Never, never turn a loaf of bread upside down.

SLEEPING

42. Never sleep with your head at the foot of the bed; this is surely fatal.
43. Don't sing in bed.
44. A man should never dream of a naked woman; a woman should never dream of a naked man. (You know who you are . . .)

MISCELLANEOUS

45. Try not to imagine it's Saturday when it's not.
46. Never sell a dog.
47. Don't even *think* about mocking an owl. ✹

Avoid all the risky things listed above — unless you're wearing this suit.

CHAPTER 10

Old Age: Days of Wisdom & Reflection

W HY IS IT that when we've finally achieved some semblance of wisdom regarding life's pleasures and sorrows; when everything we've worried about has become a small part of a far greater whole; when, based on first-hand experience, we're able at long last to provide advice on most of life's problems . . . why is it that when all of this is true, it is also true we are very old?

Oh, that life could be more like the Almanac itself. It has lived longer than any other continuously published periodical in North America, and yet it becomes stronger and healthier with every passing year. One could ask, of course, whether it's wiser from having outlasted all but one of the twelve editors it has had since 1792. (The twelfth, incidentally, is feeling just fine, thank you.) In other words, as it enters its third century of existence, does it indeed emulate those readers who represent venerable old age as a time of wisdom and reflection? Not at all. It's far too soon. Let's save that exalted state for the very last chapter. ❀

No matter the age, let the swinging times continue!

How to Become Immortal

Undying fame — or disgrace — can be had by a person whose name becomes an eponym, a part of the language. For example . . .

By Tim Clark

BLOOMERS

AMELIA BLOOMER (1818–1894) was editor of the *Lily*, an American feminist newspaper. Her enthusiastic promotion of Elizabeth Smith Miller's fashion bombshell made her name synonymous with the loose, baggy pantaloons for women that one critic claimed would land wearers "in the lunatic asylum or perchance the state prison."

CONDOMS

Legend has it that someone in the court of the rakish Charles II of England — a man named Condom — devised the prophylactic from animal intestines. Giovanni Casanova (1725–1798), an eponym himself, is said to have been a customer.

DERRICK

Godfrey Derrick (or Derick) was a soldier in the service of Robert, Earl of Essex, in the sixteenth century. Convicted of rape, Derrick was pardoned by Essex, who made him an executioner at Tyburn, outside London. Derrick became so well known that the gallows, and later any kind of hoisting machine, came to be known as a derrick. In 1601, Essex himself was executed — by Godfrey Derrick (perhaps the origin of the exclamation "By Godfrey!").

EIFFEL TOWER

Gustave Eiffel (1832–1923) was a French engineer who designed what was then the world's tallest structure for the Paris Exposition of 1889. He was also responsible for the interior framework of the Statue of Liberty.

GUILLOTINE

Joseph Guillotin (1738–1814) did not invent the decapitation machine that bears his name, nor did he lose his head to it, as legend claims. Guillotin, a physician and legislator during the French Revolution, merely endorsed the use of the machine invented by one of his colleagues, Dr. Antoine Louis, as a more humane method of execution than hanging. Later on, Guillotin's family petitioned the French government to change the name of the device. The government suggested that the family change *its* name instead.

OPPOSITE: Joseph Guillotin didn't invent this deadly contraption. But he acquired a peculiar immortality when the device was given his name. (Actually, the one shown here is a trick, two-bladed version used by magicians.)

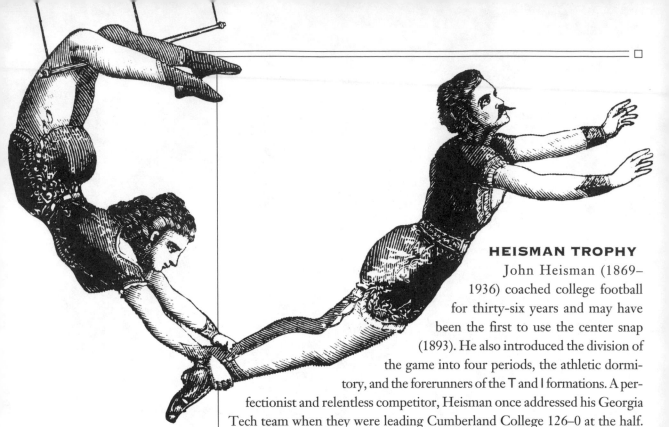

Jules Leotard not only invented the garment that's named for him, but also became the first man to perform a somersault on the flying trapeze.

HEISMAN TROPHY

John Heisman (1869–1936) coached college football for thirty-six years and may have been the first to use the center snap (1893). He also introduced the division of the game into four periods, the athletic dormitory, and the forerunners of the T and I formations. A perfectionist and relentless competitor, Heisman once addressed his Georgia Tech team when they were leading Cumberland College 126–0 at the half. "Men, we're in front, but you never know what those Cumberland players have up their sleeves," Heisman told his team. "Don't let up." Tech won 222–0, earning the coach the nickname "Shut the Gates of Mercy" Heisman.

IMMELMANN TURN

This aerial combat maneuver, in which a pilot pulls his plane up sharply in a loop that brings him down on his pursuer's tail, was invented by German fighter ace Max Immelmann (1890–1916) during World War I. It didn't prevent him from being shot down and killed in a dogfight.

JOSH

Josh Billings, the pen name of Henry Wheeler Shaw (1818–1885), was a New England humorist, and some authorities believe that the word *joshing* can be traced to his popular jokes and stories. Others disagree, bringing to mind one of Billings's favorite sayings: "It is better to know nothing than to know what ain't so."

KINSEY REPORT

Alfred Charles Kinsey (1894–1956) was the world's leading authority on the gall wasp when he turned his attention to a new subject — human sexuality. His two reports — *Sexual Behavior in the Human Male* (1948) and *Sexual Behavior in the Human Female* (1953) sold hundreds of thousands of copies and inspired much debate. Ironically, the gall wasp reproduces by parthenogenesis — the male does not fertilize the female.

LEOTARD

Jules Leotard (1830–1870) was a French aerialist who not only invented the one-piece gymnastic costume but also was the first man to perform a somersault on the flying trapeze.

MARTINET

This word for a strict disciplinarian comes from Jean Martinet, an officer in the army of the French king Louis XIV. Martinet was killed in 1672 by a shot from his own men. Everyone agreed it must have been an accident.

NOBEL PRIZE

Alfred Nobel's (1833–1896) invention of dynamite and other explosives made him a fortune that he left in trust to establish prizes for peace, physics, chemistry, physiology and medicine, and literature. He saw no contradiction in this. "The day when two army corps will be able to destroy each other in one second," he wrote, "all civilized nations will recoil from war in horror and disband their armies."

PULLMAN CARS

If it hadn't been for the assassination of President Abraham Lincoln, George Pullman's (1831–1897) name would never have been associated with railroad sleeping cars. In 1863, Pullman spent every penny he owned making a luxurious sleeping car he called the Pullman *Pioneer*. Trouble was, it was too tall to fit under bridges and too wide to slide past station platforms. But in 1865, Illinois officials ordered state bridges and platforms rebuilt so that Lincoln's body could be brought home to Springfield in the finest style. General Ulysses S. Grant, who accompanied the body, liked the Pullman enough to ask for it again when he became president. Eventually, Pullman went into business with Andrew Carnegie and became a millionaire.

SIDEBURNS

Ambrose Burnside (1824–1881) went bankrupt making rifles in 1857, ordered the Union Army of the Potomac into an appalling slaughter at Fredericksburg in 1862, illegally jailed opponents of the war in Ohio, and finally left military life in disgrace after another debacle in 1864. Nevertheless, Rhode Islanders elected him to three terms as governor and then to the U.S. Senate, where he died in office. He is remembered chiefly for his long side-whiskers, called "burnsides" in his day, but later transmuted to "sideburns." ●

The fashion of sideburns, though out of favor today, owes much to the whiskers of a Union general named Ambrose Burnside.

Never Put Off to Yesterday What You Can Do Tomorrow!

A SHAGGY GEORGE STORY

If you decided to give up doing something — like smoking, for instance — that shortens life by a specific amount of time, logic would indicate you would thus lengthen your life by that same amount of time. But what if you gave up so many bad things that your life lengthening began to exceed your normal life span?

By Dwight E. Gray

*S*ECOND CHILDHOOD comes to all of us. Some people embark upon it gradually and gracefully. Others have it thrust upon them by their junior relatives. Quite a few seem to enter it directly from first childhood. But Uncle George was different. One might say quite definitely that he achieved second childhood on purpose.

It all began years ago in his hometown of Cherry Fork, Ohio. One warm June evening, just before his twentieth birthday, Uncle George accidentally wandered into a place called Gospel Hall, where an itinerant evangelist was playing a summer engagement.

Before Uncle George could plan and execute a strategic retreat, the initial phrases of the sermon lashed out on the theme of the evils of tobacco, and Uncle George's wandering thoughts were brought sharply to attention by the speaker's rhetorical query: "Young man — do you know that every cigarette you smoke shortens your life by one and three-fifths seconds?" Although "young man" clearly was meant to address the entire group, Uncle George could not escape the feeling that the evangelist's two piercing eyes and one shaking forefinger were directed solely at him.

Well . . . Uncle George, of course, didn't know any such thing. As a matter of fact, he was a somewhat retarded smoker, having only recently graduated from corn silk behind the barn to roll-your-owns behind the poolroom. He had been toying with the idea of moving up to tailor-mades on the drugstore corner, where he could smoke and whistle at girls at the same time, but the preacher's question changed all that.

Uncle George ran for home and, once there, threw himself into the task of calculating just how much he could lengthen his life by not smoking cigarettes. He assumed that probably he would have evolved into a pack-a-day smoker, and the results of his computations staggered him. About this time, it occurred to him that a sizable fraction of cigarette addicts double in cigar and pipe smoking. Correspondence with antitobacco societies provided him with data on which to base further life-extension calculations.

While working late at night on his no-tobacco estimates, Uncle George developed the habit of taking an occasional snort of bourbon to help him stay awake. Then one day, in the then-current issue of *The Youth's Companion*, he saw a two-column cut showing a grim-faced cleric whose eyes and pointing finger were dead ringers for those of the antitobacco evangelist. This man was saying, "Think of it, young people — just one little drink of Demon Rum's devilish brew takes three and one-third seconds off your life!" Uncle George was appalled. Here he had been tippling away the precious hours

OPPOSITE: *Like Uncle George in this story, Peter Pan (here portrayed by Mary Martin) proved one need never grow up.*

Longing for the Old Mud Pies

By Florence A. Jones

Down in a little back garden,
Under a sunny sky,
We made mud pies together —
My little sweetheart and I.
Stained was the little pink apron,
Muddy the jacket blue,
As we stirred and mixed and
tasted,
Out in the sun and dew.

Why do I dream of that garden,
I who am old and wise?
Why am I longing, longing
For one of those old mud pies?
Oh, for the little pink apron,
Oh, for the jacket blue,
For the blessed faith of childhood
When make-believes are true.

he had saved by not smoking. He immediately threw out his bottle and once again began the now familiar computation routine.

And so it went, with Uncle George's ever accelerating search for things he could stop doing and thereby lengthen his life. He swore off coffee. He gave up starchy foods. He stayed out of automobiles and elevators and off trains and horses. He forsook those interrelated pursuits of staying up late and going with girls. He quit helping his mother around the house. As it became increasingly difficult to find things not to do, he began to worry a lot. Then he read that worrying shortens life, so he gave that up, too.

May 1924 brought the biggest crisis of his career. In that month, Uncle George discovered that the rate at which he was extending his life exceeded that at which he would normally be living it. Every twelve months he lived, he was saving something over thirteen months. In short, he was in a state of negative aging, which meant his life history necessarily would be retraced. And so, at appropriate stages, in a reverse chronological sequence, he stopped voting, turned in his driver's license, attempted to graduate from high school prior to registering to enter the school the following fall as a senior, changed his voice from baritone to boy soprano, gave up playing in the town band and started running after it with the rest of the kids, traded in a rusty rowing machine on an Erector Set, canceled his subscription to *Captain Billy's Whiz Bang* and subscribed to *Junior Joy*, quit feeding the family cat and started throwing stones at it, and so forth. This progressive retrogression continued as Uncle George contracted the usual childhood diseases in reverse order, and climaxed when he caught the croup and died.

The tragic end came on June 13, 1959, his birthday, when he was exactly two years old on his negative aging scale. Understandably, grief at this unfortunate end to a most unusual life was mixed with a certain feeling of relief. One must recognize, however, that overshadowing these reactions was a deep sense of frustration. His friends and relatives all had been so terribly curious as to what would have happened on June 13, 1961. ✸

Old Folks Are Worth a Fortune

The following is of unknown origin. The original was signed simply "an old gal."

REMEMBER, old folks are worth a fortune, with silver in their hair, gold in their teeth, stones in their kidneys, lead in their feet, and gas in their stomachs.

I have become a little older since I saw you last, and a few changes have come into my life since then. Frankly, I have become quite a frivolous old gal. I am seeing five gentlemen every day. As soon as I wake up, Will Power helps me get out of bed. Then I go to see John. Then Charlie Horse comes along, and when he is here, he takes a lot of my time and attention. When he leaves, Arthur Ritis shows up and stays the rest of the day. He doesn't like to stay in one place very long, so he takes me from joint to joint. After such a busy day, I'm really tired and glad to go to bed with Ben Gay. What a life!

P.S. The preacher came to call the other day. He said at my age I should be thinking about the here-after. I told him, "Oh, I do all the time. No matter where I am — in the parlor, upstairs, in the kitchen, or down in the basement — I ask myself, 'Now, what am I here after?' "

Courtesy of A. Foster, Versailles, Kentucky.

She spends her days with Arthur Ritis, sleeps with Ben Gay.

A wise man hath more ballast than sail.

– 1943 –

The Amazing Longevity of Our Founding Fathers

In 1775, a mere 2 percent of the populace was over 65. And yet our first 10 presidents lived an average of 77.4 years. Why? Therein may lie important advice for us all.

BY LAWRENCE DOORLEY

CAN A PERSON be too busy to die? Can a vital undertaking be so engrossing that there is just no time to answer the door when doomsday comes knocking? Not likely, say the geneticists, insisting that the length of one's life is mainly determined by how long his or her ancestors lived.

But Dr. Kenneth Pelletier, authority on longevity, disputes the geneticists. "Good genes give you an edge," Dr. Pelletier admits, "but that doesn't account for people who live thirty to forty years beyond average life expectancy. A strong sense of purpose, commitment to higher values, as well as lifelong physical and mental activity play a more important role in longevity than purely biological factors such as hormonal changes." He asserts that the single most important predictor of longevity is enthusiasm for life: staying busy, being curious, feeling that you are accomplishing something worthwhile.

Proof that the "too busy to die" theory is more than wishful thinking can be found in the long and productive lives of the founding fathers. Life expectancy at birth in Colonial America between 1700 and 1775 was 35 years (today it is 72.0 for men and 78.8 for women). But since life expectancy is defined as the number of years an individual of a given age may expect on the average to live, once the colonial American reached 21, odds favored his living another 20 years. And the longer one lived, the better the chance of living to a ripe old age.

Nevertheless, in 1775 a mere 2 percent of the populace was over 65. Yet an amazing number of founding fathers, all born in the perilous eighteenth century, achieved a longevity far beyond the average.

Our first ten presidents — Washington through Tyler — lived an average of 77.4 years, while our last ten deceased presidents — William Howard Taft through Richard Nixon (excluding John Kennedy, whose early death would further lower the average) — lived an average of only 72 years.

> It is every man's duty to make himself profitable to mankind; if he can, to many; if not, to fewer; if not so either, to his neighbors; but, however, to himself.
>
> – 1807 –

Of the fifty-six signers of the Declaration of Independence, three lived to 90 or beyond (Charles Carroll of Maryland lived to 95); nine more to 80 or beyond; an additional eight to 70 or more; and another sixteen reached 60 or more. Benjamin Franklin lived to 84, Paul Revere to 83, Noah Webster to 85, John Jay to 84, Samuel Adams to 81, Charles Bulfinch to 81, John Trumbull to 87, and John Marshall to 80.

Some might argue that the founders must have had long-lived ancestors (some did, but most didn't), a privileged background (fewer than half did), or superior medical care (it didn't exist for anyone, rich or poor).

Perhaps Benjamin Franklin had the best formula for achieving longevity. In his twenties, he compiled a list of Thirteen Virtues that would govern his life. Virtue 6 was Industry: "Lose no time; be always employ'd in something useful; cut off all unnecessary actions."

There it is: the founding fathers were industrious. They schemed, harangued, wrote, organized, fought — many of them in bloody battles — to free the colonies. Then, while some of them worked furiously to prevent the unhewn nation from falling apart, others rushed back to the workshop to pick up their tools. They were a diverse group: aristocrats, common

A Little Poem Found on a Scrap of Paper in Our Old Dresser Drawer

God has given us two ends
With a common link.
With the one we sit;
With the other we think.
Success in life depends
Which we choose:
Heads you win;
Tails you lose.

sorts; college graduates, autodidacts; short-tempered, imperturbable; neat, sloppy; stingy, generous. Some smoked; most drank moderately, mainly wine. Some exercised diligently, others halfheartedly. But they all had one thing in common: they saw life as a heaven-sent gift, a gift to be used, not wasted, not squandered.

Why don't we all try this? See how it works out. ✸

FIRST 10 U.S. PRESIDENTS

	BORN	DIED	AGE
George Washington	2-22-1732	12-14-1799	67
John Adams	10-30-1735	7-4-1826	90
Thomas Jefferson	4-13-1743	7-4-1826	83
James Madison	3-16-1751	6-28-1836	85
James Monroe	4-28-1758	7-4-1831	73
John Quincy Adams	7-11-1767	2-23-1848	80
Andrew Jackson	3-15-1767	6-8-1845	78
Martin Van Buren	12-5-1782	7-24-1862	79
William Henry Harrison	2-9-1773	4-4-1841	68
John Tyler	3-29-1790	1-18-1862	71
Average age at death:			77.4

LAST 10 DECEASED PRESIDENTS

(excluding John F. Kennedy)

	BORN	DIED	AGE
William Howard Taft	9-15-1857	3-8-1930	72
Woodrow Wilson	12-29-1856	2-3-1924	67
Warren G. Harding	11-2-1865	8-2-1923	57
Calvin Coolidge	7-4-1872	1-5-1933	60
Herbert Hoover	8-10-1874	10-20-1964	90
Franklin D. Roosevelt	1-30-1882	4-12-1945	63
Harry S Truman	5-8-1884	12-26-1972	88
Dwight D. Eisenhower	10-14-1890	3-28-1969	78
Lyndon B. Johnson	8-27-1908	1-22-1973	64
Richard M. Nixon	1-9-1913	4-22-1994	81
Average age at death:			72.0

> To combat senility and loss of mental vigor, drink two teaspoons of apple cider vinegar in a glass of water at least twice a day.
>
> — 19TH CENTURY —

The Old Farmer's Almanac Book of Everyday Advice

What Will the Future Bring?

For the 1979 Almanac, we asked author/musician/
philosopher/artist/scientist/stonemason/educator/octogenarian
(and Almanac contributor for many years)
Guy Murchie what he saw beyond
the forthcoming millennium.

By Guy Murchie

I HAVE NO PARTICULAR credentials as a prophet. But somehow I sense the inadequacy of trying to predict the unknown future by extrapolating from the known past. This sense helps me to visualize a future that is, in many respects, unrelated to the past.

Most obvious is the approaching period of severe famine and deprivation that cannot but increase. Starvation will inevitably become widespread on earth during droughts in undeveloped and overpopulated tropical regions. But by some time in the twenty-first century, if my surmise is right, people will, for the first time, make the sacrifices and decisions resulting in the disarming of all nations. And the ensuing relaxation of tensions will doubtless enhance harmony among all people. At the same time, a world monetary system will stabilize commerce. And a standardized world language, taught in schools on every continent, will increase understanding.

Although economic and political synthesis must exert a conservative influence on our progress in the next century, our technological ingenuity need not be so restrained. In fact, that is where the earth's most dramatic changes can be expected.

- Within a millennium or two, there may even be tunnels straight through the molten heart of the earth, using natural gravitational power to convey cargoes and passengers anywhere on the surface in 42.2 minutes (that being half the 84.4-minute period of a Schuler pendulum or a satellite orbiting the planet), the 42 minutes made up of falling downward in frictionless acceleration for 21 minutes, then coasting upward again in frictionless deceleration for another 21 minutes according to the earth's natural harmonics.

- Next century, fusion power will be used, among other things, for desalting ocean water in massive quantities, and saline agriculture (using seawater) will grow phenomenally in some areas.

- Medical research is actively studying artificial vision, hearing, smelling, and so on for the sensorially deprived by way of brain waves electroni-

>
> Experience is
> what enables you
> to recognize a
> mistake when you
> make it again.
>
> – 1947 –

Remember the Human Coping Mechanism

COMMENTING ON ALL THE CURRENT prophecies of doom (and all prophecies down through the centuries have usually been of the doom variety), historian Barbara Tuchman said, "You cannot extrapolate any series in which the human element intrudes; that is, the human narrative never follows and will always fool the scientific curve . . . the doom factor sooner or later generates a coping mechanism."

Protesters find their own way to cope with World War I.

cally shaped by sensory instruments and channeled into the visual, auditory, and olfactory centers of the brain. And it has made dramatic progress in the repair, replacement, and improvement of body parts, which means grafting on either artificial organs or natural tissue from another spot if not another body, or possibly inducing the same body to regenerate itself as does a worm.

• Physicist Gerard K. O'Neill of Princeton proposes harnessing cheap, plentiful solar power in space by building huge, parabolic mirrors there to collect heat and generate electric power to be beamed to earth. The construction crews and permanent operators (with their families) also will live in space in great cylindrical "pieces of earth." These will be a mile in circumference and perhaps half a mile long, containing towns of up to ten thousand people nestled amid wooded farmland with ponds, fish, birds, flowers, atmosphere — everything that might promote a fulfilling life, including earth-strength "gravity" provided by rotating the cylinders. Power for the space towns will be generated in pollution-free solar panels between the movable mirrors that will direct sunlight inward for any agreed number of hours per "day," regulating "weather" and "seasons" to common need.

• More ambitious, in the sense of looking ahead not just thousands but actually millions of years, is the elaborate proposal of another Princeton physicist, Freeman Dyson, of the famous Institute for Advanced Study, and former chairman of the Federation of American Scientists. Dyson believes that an advanced planetary race like humans must, in time, redesign and rearrange the entire solar system, not only commandeering its moons and asteroids and reorbiting or towing them about with powerful "space tugs," but even dismantling the giant planets such as Jupiter and Saturn and steering asteroid-size chunks of them into orbits nearer the sun. There, he says, they will soon warm up and be made to fall together into moonish spheres that can be tailored into hospitable annexes for expanding human life, eventually forming a kind of doughnut ring of thousands of small, inhabited "planets," using appropriate asteroids as mines for needed minerals, fertilizing some as nurseries or laboratories, rigging others for solar energy.

- I think the earth's cities will continue to grow (at a slowing rate), at least into the twenty-first century. By this time, megalopolises will have spread in crystalline patterns for thousands of miles across North America, Europe, Japan, China, and India, extending even through parts of Africa, South America, and Australia.

- But the countermovement (away from concrete and asphalt) will be developing too (at a faster rate), increasing wooded park areas in ratio to city populations, humanizing housing, creating giant automated cities like Babelnoah (designed by Paolo Soleri for six million people) and the huge, mobile, floating ones (promoted by Buckminster Fuller) that may begin to populate the oceans any decade now. And there will be a wide spectrum of planned villages where everybody can go fishing, or to shops or church, and where children can walk to school without crossing any streets.

IN CONCLUSION . . .

Of course, it is impossible for any mere human to know the distant future with any certitude, but I cannot help feeling that the familiar think-tank approach to prediction has stressed future technology overmuch in its extrapolation of the obvious accelerations of the recent past, while almost no one mentions the less obvious coming of spiritual maturity that (to me) seems overdue. Many reject out of hand the concept of God as an intelligent humanlike being, but I am convinced that any deep-thinking person will ultimately admit that there must be tremendous forces dominating this universe, which are hidden and unknowable to us, therefore essentially mysterious and in effect playing the part of a supreme being.

In consequence, as science and religion intermittently continue to merge toward a rational synthesis, the ancient hypothesis of divinity must sooner or later also regain acceptance as science reaches beyond the tangibility of matter that physicists now explain as waves of energy and into the measurable cousinhood of all creatures from worms to stars — to the eventual realization that our mortal life on earth in essence constitutes a school for evolving souls. Indeed, this is a school in which the rapidly evolving human spirit is in perpetual transcendence from terrestrial finitude (using the tools of space, time, and self) to the greater life of infinitude (beyond all tools) outside the shell of death. ❀

A minister who had once been a printer observed in one of his sermons that "youth might be compared to a comma, manhood to a semicolon, old age to a colon, to which death puts a period."

– 1854 –

A Farmer's Last Will

The following was sent to the Almanac by Arthur Morris, a pecan farmer from Broken Arrow, Oklahoma.

I LEAVE: To my wife, my overdraft at the bank — maybe she can explain it.

To my banker, my soul — he has the mortgage on it anyway.

To my neighbor, my clown suit — he'll need it if he continues to farm as he has in the past.

To the county agent, fifty bushels of corn to see if he can hit the market — I never could.

To the junk man, all my machinery — he's had his eye on it for years.

To my undertaker, a special request — I want six implement and fertilizer dealers for my pallbearers. They're all used to carrying me.

To the weatherman, rain and sleet and snow for the funeral, please — no sense having good weather now.

To the gravedigger — don't bother. The hole I'm in should be big enough.

TEXT CREDITS

Grateful acknowledgment is made to the following for permission to reprint previously published material.

David Archie: "What to Say When You're Selling Your House" by David Archie from the 1986 edition of *The Old Farmer's Almanac.* Reprinted with permission of the author.

Earle Barnhart: "How to Weed Your Garden for Chicken Feed," originally published as "Chickens as Garden Helpers," by Earle Barnhart from the 1992 edition of *The Old Farmer's Almanac.* Reprinted with permission of the author.

Francelia Butler: "Rope Skipping Across America" by Francelia Butler from the 1990 edition of *The Old Farmer's Almanac.* Reprinted with permission of the author.

Carol Publishing Group: 17 insults from *2000 Insults for All Occasions* by Louis A. Safian. Copyright © 1965 by Louis A. Safian. Published by arrangement with Carol Publishing Group. A Citadel Press Book.

Suki Casanave: "Practical Advice on Becoming a World Record Holder," originally published as "How to Become a World Record Holder," by Suki Casanave from the 1993 edition of *The Old Farmer's Almanac.* Reprinted with permission of the author.

Jim Collins: "Turn Over, Dear, For God's Sake, Turn Over!" by Jim Collins from the 1991 edition of *The Old Farmer's Almanac.* Reprinted with permission of the author.

Lawrence Doorley: "The Amazing Longevity of Our Founding Fathers" by Lawrence Doorley from the 1994 edition of *The Old Farmer's Almanac.* Reprinted with permission of the author.

Castle Freeman: "On the Subject of Fireplace Wood" by Castle Freeman from the 1991 edition of *The Old Farmer's Almanac,* plus excerpts from the 1989, 1990, 1992, 1993 Farmer's Essays

in *The Old Farmer's Almanac.* Reprinted with permission of the author.

Judy Gorman: "The True Nature of Crumpets" by Judy Gorman from the 1990 edition of *The Old Farmer's Almanac.* Reprinted with permission of the author.

Lael J. Littke: "Why It's Not Advisable to Name a Cow After Your Neighbor's Wife" by Lael J. Littke from the 1992 edition of *The Old Farmer's Almanac.* Reprinted with permission of the author.

Donella H. Meadows: "If the World Were a Village of 1,000 People . . ." by Donella H. Meadows from the 1992 edition of *The Old Farmer's Almanac.* Reprinted with permission of the author.

Guy Murchie: "What Will the Future Bring?" by Guy Murchie from the 1992 edition of *The Old Farmer's Almanac.* Reprinted with permission of the author.

Deborah Navas: "On Behalf of Bulldog Gravy" by Deborah Navas from the 1991 edition of *The Old Farmer's Almanac.* Reprinted with permission of the author.

The Reader's Digest Association, Inc.: "How Long Will You Live?" from *Practical Problem Solver,* copyright © 1991 by The Reader's Digest Association, Inc. Reprinted by permission.

Stan Schirmacher: "18 Rules for Good Riting" by Stan Schirmacher from the 1975 edition of *The Old Farmer's Almanac.* Reprinted with permission of the author.

Bob Trebilcock: "Everything You Always Wanted to Know About Cheesecake" by Bob Trebilcock from the 1989 edition of *The Old Farmer's Almanac.* Reprinted with permission of the author.

Robert Tubbesing: "Intimate Wisdom from Wadsworth, Ohio," originally published as "Pearls of Wisdom from the Heart of the Midwest," by Robert Tubbesing from the 1986 edition of *The Old Farmer's Almanac.* Reprinted with permission of the author.

Jon Vara: "The Case for Weeding in the Dark" by Jon Vara from the 1991 edition of *The Old Farmer's Almanac.* Reprinted with permission of the author.

PICTURE CREDITS

Page ii: Dover Publications.

Chapter One. Pages 2–3: Culver Pictures. Pages 4–5, 6: Photofest. Page 7: Dover Publications. Page 8: Photofest. Page 9: H. Armstrong Roberts. Page 10: Yankee Archives. Page 11: Foto Marburg/Art Resource, New York. Page 12: Culver Pictures. Pages 14–15: Dover Publications. Page 16: Yankee Archives. Page 17 (clockwise from top left): Culver Pictures, Archive Photos, Culver Pictures, Yankee Archives. Page 18: H. Armstrong Roberts. Page 19: The Bettmann Archive. Page 21: Archive Photos/Kamp. Page 22: H. Armstrong Roberts. Pages 24 (both), 25, 26: Jill Shaffer. Page 27: Culver Pictures. Page 28: Photofest. Page 29: Culver Pictures. Page 30: FPG International. Page 31: Robert W. Young/FPG International.

Chapter Two. Pages 32–33: FPG International. Page 35: H. Armstrong Roberts. Pages 36, 37: Yankee Archives. Page 38: Dover Publications. Page 39: H. Armstrong Roberts. Pages 40–41: The Detroit Historical Museum. Pages 42, 43: Dover Publications. Page 44: Bob Taylor/FPG International. Page 47: Cape Cod Pilgrim Memorial Association, Provincetown, Massachusetts. Pages 48–49, 50: Ann Card. Page 51: H. Armstrong Roberts. Page 53: Drawing by George Price, © 1953, 1981 The New Yorker Magazine, Inc.

Chapter Three. Pages 54–55: Photofest. Page 56: Archive Photos/ Lambert. Page 57: H. Armstrong Roberts. Page 58: Photo by Paul Ehrenfest, courtesy American Institute of Physics/Emilio Segrè Visual Archives. Page 59: Courtesy American Antiquarian Society. Page 60 (top, both): Culver

Pictures. Page 60 (bottom): SNOOPY reprinted by permission of UFS, Inc. Page 61: Hard Times Collectibles, P.O. Box 5222, Santa Cruz, CA 95063. Pages 62–63: Yankee Archives. Page 64: Dover Publications. Page 65: Detail, Collections of the Maine Historical Society. Page 67: FPG International. Page 68: The Bettmann Archive. Page 69: Dover Publications. Page 70: Simone Martini, Workshop of, *Saint James Major*, Samuel H. Kress Collection, © 1994 National Gallery of Art, Washington, D.C. Page 71: From *Mythology* by Edith Hamilton, © 1942 by Edith Hamilton, © renewed 1966 by Dorian Fielding Reid and Doris Fielding, by permission of Little, Brown and Company.

Chapter Four. Pages 72–73: Culver Pictures. Page 75: Library of Congress LC–USZ62–80310. Page 77: Photofest. Page 78: Dover Publications. Page 79 (both): from *Familiar Trees and their Leaves* by F. Schuyler Mathews, New York, 1901. Page 80: Yankee Archives. Page 82: Dover Publications. Page 83: Culver Pictures. Pages 84–85: Detail, National Gallery of Canada, Ottawa, transfer from the Canadian War Memorials, 1921 (Gift of the 2nd Duke of Westminster, Eaton Hall, Cheshire, 1918).

Chapter Five. Pages 86–87: F.D.R. Library. Pages 88–89: Advertisement used by permission from Campbell Soup Company. Page 90: Dover Publications. Page 91: Yankee Archives. Pages 92, 94 (bottom): H. Armstrong Roberts. Page 94 (top): Dover Publications. Page 95: H. Armstrong Roberts. Page 96: Private Collection. Page 97: Yankee Archives. Page 98: FPG International. Page 99: Reprinted with the permission of Charles Scribner's Sons, an imprint of Macmillan Publishing Company, from *The Black Arrow* by Robert Louis Stevenson, illustrated by N.C. Wyeth, © 1916 Charles Scribner's Sons, © renewed 1944 by N.C.

Wyeth. Page 101: Private Collection. Pages 102, 103: Dover Publications.

Chapter Six. Pages 106–07, 109: H. Armstrong Roberts. Page 110 (all): Susan Dunholter. Page 111 (top): Jill Shaffer. Page 111 (bottom): Karnan/ FPG International. Page 112: FPG International. Page 113: Susan Dunholter. Pages 114–15: Archive Photos/Lambert. Page 117: Photofest. Pages 118, 119: Yankee Archives. Page 121: Archive Photos/Hirz. Page 122: Dover Publications. Page 123: H. Armstrong Roberts. Page 124: Yankee Archives. Page 125: Hercules Incorporated. Page 126: Photofest. Pages 128–29: H. Armstrong Roberts.

Chapter Seven. Pages 130–31: H. Armstrong Roberts. Page 133: Photofest. Pages 134–35: Image # 901, Lee Moorhouse Collection, Special Collections, University of Oregon Library. Page 136: Yankee Archives. Page 138: Movie Still Archive/FPG International. Page 139: Centennial Gift of Landon T. Clay, courtesy Museum of Fine Arts, Boston. Pages 140, 141: Dover Publications. Page 142: Private Collection. Page 144: Detail, Archives of American Art, Smithsonian Institution, neg. #CC07, Charles Caffin Papers, photograph by Frances Benjamin Johnston. Page 145: Archive Photos/ Lambert. Page 147: Courtesy the Collection of E. Morgan Williams, P.O. Box 2607, Washington, DC 20013. Page 148: Photofest.

Chapter Eight. Pages 150–51: Circus World Museum, Baraboo, Wisconsin. Page 152: Archive Photos. Page 153: Bruce Hammond. Page 154: Archive Photos/Lohse. Page 155: Sherry White/courtesy *Cartertet News Times*. Pages 156, 157: Culver Pictures. Pages 158, 159: AP/Wide World Photos. Page 160: Dover Publications. Page 161: Photo by H.H. Bennett, courtesy of Bennett Studio Foundation. Page 162: H. Armstrong Roberts. Page 163: The

Bettmann Archive. Page 165: Culver Pictures. Pages 166–67: Dover Publications. Page 168: Photofest. Page 169: Archive Photos/Lambert. Page 170: Yankee Archives. Page 171: H. Armstrong Roberts. Page 173: FPG International.

Chapter Nine. Pages 174–75: Archive Photos/Lambert. Page 177: Archive Photos/Herbert. Pages 178, 179: Photofest. Page 180: The Kansas State Historical Society, Topeka, Kansas. Page 182: Photofest. Page 183: DeWitt Historical Society of Tompkins County, Ithaca, New York. Page 185: Photofest. Page 186: Archive Photos/Lambert. Page 187: Neg. no. 315110, courtesy Department of Library Services, American Museum of Natural History. Page 189: Gotham Book Mart, Inc., New York, New York. Page 191: FPG International.

Chapter Ten. Pages 192–93: Archive Photos/Lambert. Page 195: FPG International. Pages 196, 197: Dover Publications. Page 198: Photofest. Page 200: FPG International. Page 201: H. Armstrong Roberts. Page 203: Courtesy Winterthur Museum. Page 204: Alinari/Art Resource, New York. Page 206: Culver Pictures. Page 208: FPG International. Page 210: from *The Depression Years as Photographed by Arthur Rothstein*, Dover Publications, 1978.

Note: Diligence was exercised in locating owners of all images used. If an image was uncredited or mistakenly credited, please contact the publisher and effort will be made to include credit in future printings.